QUEEN CALLED BITCH

Tales of a Teenage Bitter-Ass Homosexual

Waldell Goode

Published by
NineStar Press
PO Box 91792
Albuquerque, New Mexico, 87199
www.ninestarpress.com

Print ISBN #978-1-947139-47-3
Cover by Natasha Snow
Edited by Jason Bradley

To Reed Morris, for the unique way you bicker me back to sanity.

Acknowledgements

I have to thank an unyielding God for seeing this dream into reality. Daniel Ellis, my first true fan, and without whom, this book could've easily wasted away in a file folder I never would've checked twice. The Dimaanos for who they are. Every teacher, mentor, family member, stranger who told me to "do." My mother, one thousand times over. I know strength and resilience because I know her. And my sisters Crystal, Amber, and Tatayanna—you are my foundation. I would not bother existing without the three of you. Oh, and Mrs. Hamilton for failing me in chemistry. Yes, you were right!

Preface

You have to know who you are in order to find the joy in the work you have yet to do.
– Debbie Allen

Let me preface this by proclaiming to you, I don't know anything. I don't know politically correct terms, I'm not absolutely sure about the advances of any "gay agenda," I'm not sure what offends people or what could be taken as offensive, and I am most certainly not sure of exactly who I am. I've been struggling with this question since the day I was born, and I've been in dire frustration trying to figure me out ever since.

That being said, there are a few things I'm absolutely positive of—my mother loves me, God is real, and Reba McEntire is a musical goddess who will sing beautiful melodies as Jesus Christ descends from the clouds in the midst of the rapture. I know I'm beautiful. I know I love me. I know that I'm lonely, and yes, loneliness sucks shit sometimes, especially when you can't ignore it anymore. I know I will make it in life even if it's merely by the skin of my teeth, and I know I can't bear to think otherwise. The reason why I present the aforementioned introspections as truths is because they are largely beliefs. Beliefs are beautiful because no one can take those away from you. If you believe something that can't be disputed, why not embrace these prevailing thoughts as realities?

Okay, so that was innately bad advice—that's how idiots are created. I'm sure Bill O'Reilly believes he's smart and is taken seriously as a political commentator, Sarah Palin believes governing Alaska really means something, and One Million Moms believe they are *not* bigots. However, this isn't about fucktards who still don't seem to grasp basic concepts of Civil Rights; this is about a queen called bitch struggling to discover who he is in rural America, or Hell as the more informed identify it. So, in reference to beliefs, maybe there's some middle ground. Beliefs, as I profess them to be, are fundamental thoughts that provide individuals a safe house of ideas and moral reckoning, allowing them to further act in good conscience—or conversely, to justify acts by manipulating said ideas to supplement one's choices. Let's hope mine are the good, conscience kind.

In all that I know, and even more so in all that I *don't* know, life sucks. I mean, it fucking sucks. Objectively speaking, I've lived a great life. I was never abused. My father, uncle, cousins, mother, sisters, or aunts never tried to rape me, no Academy Award winning material here, but I know I'm not who I used to be. I'm not the person who dreams endlessly, or always has a smile, or even wishes someone well like I used to. I'm not the happy queen in the corner, distributing cookies and motherly advice like I'm Mother Theresa with a penis, speaking words of optimistic promise while encouraging someone to fall in love with every breath they take. I'm more of the person telling someone to just survive the best way they can, and that's no way to live. Even Tarzan had Jane, that lucky bitch (Jane, not Tarzan).

Even though I've never passed out baked goods and the only mother I remotely resemble is Mother Nature (because I wouldn't flinch while making a bitch bleed), I will be the first to say I need a better me. The reason why I'm writing this, is I feel that going through my past and examining beliefs I strongly support or reject will provide adequate insight as to who I am or where I went wrong. I also realize I have somewhat of a vulnerability issue, and this is a way I can express who I am, safely behind the comfort of my computer screen wrapped in my Snuggie. So kick back, audience of one—more likely none—it's time to discover the real Princess WaWa, a subject I'm sure consumes your every waking thought because I'm that important. Soon, I hope to discover why I am a queen called bitch, and these are my tales as a teenage bitter-ass homosexual...

One: Ryan Murphy's a Fucking Liar

I officially begin with this because it is one of the more poignant issues I've been dealing with. It's not that I have anything against *Glee*. I applaud the nature and success of the series, but I dislike how certain plot points, characters, storylines, and adolescent relationships deviate from realities concurrent with that of the authentic experience of my life. *Glee* is an excellent series, bringing awareness all across America of certain groups that have been neglected or outcast in a universal school setting. There isn't any show that has mastered such a feat at the level *Glee* has, which is why the series remains a phenomenon, reaching and inspiring children all over the world to be themselves and embrace each other's differences. Unless they're Asian, in which case they're promptly reminded to remain silent and take their proper places in the background where they belong; it's amazing they're allowed to consider themselves series regulars and not simply extras. I hate what they did with the token Asian character, Tina. They tried making her a more prominent character later in the series, failing miserably.

Reflecting on *Glee*, I would say their portrayal of high school is fairly accurate minus the students who appear to be better suited for an AARP commercial. I would even say my high school career was somewhat similar to Kurt's, the token gay character. I was unsure of myself freshman year. I spent my time mostly in solitude, trying to avoid much of the ridicule I received in my eighth grade year. I was involved with the drama team where I met fellow weirdos like myself, I was hiding the fact that I'm gay, and I unwittingly thought no one knew it—despite how blatantly obvious it was, and everyone else must have been previously enlightened.

Sophomore year was even better. People began to know me and who I was, that I wasn't a predator and spiritually intertwined with Satan. I came out as completely gay that year. Even I wasn't buying the bisexual nonsense I fed myself and others in years past. I began to dress as I so desired and fully embraced the inner, gayer me. Being involved with the local university's theater department, I had become acquainted with more degenerates who celebrated abnormality.

Junior year was when I finally came into my own. I led the drama department to a couple of victories as I was cast in the main role, and attended the Governor's School of Southside Virginia Community College. I enjoyed myself the most that year, even though Governor's School was stressful as hell and I failed chemistry. Senior year, the focus was on finding money to attend a university or college, and that didn't happen so I suppose one could consider that a failure, but I considered it an opportunity to fuck around for another semester.

My high school career, one could say, was excellent and probably everything it was supposed to be. A necessary step in my life, but I can't seem to shake the part about loneliness. For my senior trip at Governor's School, we went on a boat ride for an hour and a half. In a tiny vessel meant for maybe eight to seat comfortably were crammed fifteen people shoulder to shoulder, stuffing packed lunches into their mouths as the tour guide blabbed on and on about the three foot deep lake that takes twenty minutes to travel from shore to shore. Rounding the trip for the fourth or fifth time, my English teacher, sitting beside me, established conversation as a means to keep me either from sleeping, or hauling my ass overboard. Our discussion grew from her love of animals to my high school experience, to her decades—long marriage with her husband of infinite years, and on to the scandal of her marrying her old high school principal. She asked me the one question everyone in my high school career managed to avoid, ignore, or already know the answer to. It was remarkable. Before that moment, I had never considered it. I wanted to contemplate the depth of my relations, possibly due to a lack of allowing myself to ponder the grim truth of deeply rooted negative dispositions I choose to utilize as defense mechanisms.

She looked me in the eye and leaned in close. "Waldell, are you lonely?" She spoke as if she was asking about the weather.

Although we were gently gliding atop a lake and I had consumed two bottles of water with my complimentary lunch, my mouth ran completely dry.

I took a second, regained the wind that had instantaneously been trounced out of my chest, and replied with a smooth and concrete, "No. I have amazing friends."

Somehow she knew. I could see it in her eyes. That wasn't what she was asking. She would clarify, and there would be no way I could playfully avoid its severity or laugh it off as I had become accustomed to doing.

She looked at me with deeper expression now, and asked, "No, but Waldell, are you *really* lonely?"

I began to look away and pretend to notice an area of the lake I previously hadn't seen; we circled back for the thousandth time and nothing could've been missed. I couldn't avoid it. I couldn't make it funny, laugh it off, reference my mother or her alcoholism. I could only be honest with my professor, and in doing so, stop lying to myself. This is the one instance I can recall when lighthearted commentary failed to enter my mind when I needed some sort of comical relief... or relief in general. I looked her in the eye again, and with all the gusto I could find out there on the lake with sixty other people strolling along the pier, going about their day, eating their triangularly shaped cold cuts, I told myself the truth for the first time in four years with a single word.

"Yes."

And here lies my problem with *Glee*. Kurt is an amazing character. He's beautiful, funny, witty, he has flaws, and the greatest attribute a creator may accomplish with any character is the fact he's human. I appreciated that representation of a homosexual teen in mainstream media. Before him, there weren't many who closely resembled *me*. Friends and family who were familiar with the show deemed me "black Kurt," or "Blurt." I admired him, the character, his weakness and ultimate triumph over an oppressive society. As Oprah taught the world, one of the singular greatest gifts a person in the media can give is lending voice to the voiceless. That was Kurt Hummel, analogous with millions of gay teens all throughout the world, struggling to find themselves against social pressure and bullying. Kurt, portrayed by Golden Globe Award winner Chris Colfer, was a hero in a generation needing one.

I relate to this character. I understand this character; he lives in a small town, I live in small town. He knew he was gay from a very young age, and I remember when I was five and my father told my sisters they were turning me into a faggot. Kurt might as well have been real as far as character development goes. Many people felt or feel as if they know him. My biggest hindrance isn't Kurt. It's Kurt and Blaine, the boyfriend he found by transferring to a private magical school for gays only. Where was my Prince Charming, willing to stop the world and sing me thirty-two bars of a romantic cliché written nearly one hundred years ago, warning me of the freezing air outside as a means to keep me inside and eventually sleep with me? Where was my holiday crush, dying to sing a song with me made famous by a legendary songbird and famed homosexual porn star husband? Google Jack Wrangler, your life will be better because of it. I'm happy for the characters. I'm glad that it was as simple as taking a trip to Gay Land, picking out the sweetest model, and driving him back home to live out your days in happy gay bliss while each of you takes turns being more perfect. Kurt and Blaine are so wonderful, they even have sex in a special teenage special gay way, fully clothed, when Kurt loses his virginity.

Truth is, there was no guy willing to sing me anything. There isn't a school of gays you can attend while testing the waters, trying to sniff out the next Neil Patrick Harris. Chances are if you're a gay male and you're from a small town, you won't get many Prince Charmings knocking down your door, willing to make you feel special. Hell, chances are if you're a gay kid attending high school in a small town, you're probably the only gay in the vicinity—the only openly gay one, of course. Where was my romance? The best I've gotten was a thirty-eight-year-old on Grindr lusting after a minor's dirty pictures he never received. I didn't go to the prom with my boyfriend, I was never sung to or caressed in *that* way, I don't know what "I love you" means beyond friendship, my first and last kiss occurred in tenth grade and the next day the boy denied it ever happened. The only time I've ever been called attractive was by a straight bi-curious friend who considered me his "experiment" that led absolutely nowhere, and the only date I've ever been on was a non-date with a gay guy who just wasn't interested in me that way. *Glee* is astonishing, but honestly sometimes even after you've had the proper revelations and accepted yourself and others around you, life still hurts.

It's not *Glee*'s fault that I don't have anyone. I take sole responsibility. But I blame them for hope. I, along with the rest of America, cheered for Kurt and Blaine's first kiss. However, their kiss didn't make me any less alone. It's me who still cries in the middle of the night for reasons I "thought" I didn't know, but in actuality was avoiding. It's me who lives with the moment my teacher decided to get personal and made me truthful. It's me who has no one and continually decides to largely suffer in silence. How do you tell a friend, "Hey, I need you" without sounding weak? How do you admit it to yourself without remembering how painful it is? And how do you still believe in love when it has never happened to you?

I falsely call Ryan Murphy a liar, because it has never happened to me. He's deceitful because he made me forget that characters, while closely resembling real people, are fiction and their stories can have endings that include tremendous declarations of love and overwhelming displays of affection because *they're written in.* As a real gay teenager living in a real small town, I have been living the truth of what *Glee* has to avoid if only for their namesake; there is quite possibly no love story waiting for me.

Two: Cher's Crucial Question

Most gay men have heard the song. I'm willing to bet that most know it by heart and are probably singing the lyrics or humming the tune right now. Cher's "Believe" has always been more than a song for me. As it has been to many gay men before me, it's an anthem declaring strength and beauty in surviving past loves. A strength so fierce it resembles Cher's vocal cords, not an effort easily mastered. In this song, its allure, its powerful chant resounding endlessly throughout one's soul—empowering us note by note to celebrate each other's inner strength—lies a simple question that has tormented me since the moment I stumbled upon Cher's Pandora station. It's not that I don't know my answer; it's that I don't care too much for the answer I'd supply when personally addressed with the question. Silly as it may be, when Cher asked whether or not I believe in life after—you know how it goes, I felt like the only homo in the world singing this song and thinking in response, "No." I mean, I'm sure just now I broke a gay law or something.

I'm *not* sure when I first realized the unfortunate response that revealed so much about who I am. It wasn't the entire question that befuddled me. I believe in life after love. I believe in life after anything. I'm a black gay man. If there's one thing I should excel at, it's surviving. What I understood from Cher's multi-platinum single is that I don't think I believe in love. At least not for myself—I'm almost certain it happens for other people. Perhaps I'm the only one undeserving, not needing, or incapable of love. Like a true American, I've formed my ideas of love and relationships from my parents and the culture surrounding me. My parents divorced when I was extremely young, and considering 49 percent of marriages end in divorce. First world society doesn't necessarily demonstrate the strongest example of respectful unions. Furthermore, all my life I've learned silent lessons about how love damages the spirit. It does not uplift or enrich one's essence of being.

Although I was very young and don't remember my parents' breakup, I sure as hell remember the aftermath. The day my father left was the day my mother began a never-ending denouncement of his existence. Anger grew into rage, which settled into a (I wish I could say subtle) vulgar bitterness. The reasoning behind the breakup was never given in specifics, but I know it was justified and if my mother hadn't left him, I don't know where we'd be today.

My father adopted my oldest sister; she's the product of a previous relationship of my mother's, and I'm told we lived in familial bliss for seven years. As reported to me, one night my father returned home from one of his drinking excursions and inappropriately "touched" my eldest sister. In later years when I asked for further clarification, the instance being more than a decade ago, the question was still understandably unwelcome, and I failed to receive any more information regarding the topic, and honestly I didn't need much more information than I already had. Regardless, my sister was molested and it is my father's fault. It has always been that way, it always will be, and no amount of detail will ever alter that conclusion. There's no acceptable form of molestation, and knowing this, I searched for clarification simply to justify my own curiosity. In any case, my father's actions tore my mother to shreds and our family was never the same again.

Growing past such a horrid event, my sister Diamond, the survivor, strangely enough has never given up on the idea of falling in love. She loves wildly, vibrantly, fearlessly, without caution, any light-skinned, tall African-American male who's in possession of a million dollar smile. One month prior to her graduation from Norfolk State University, her boyfriend and his mother kicked her out of the apartment she and her boyfriend of five years were sharing.

Inevitably, after moving back home, anxiety set in and we all walked on eggshells in her presence. Her life at that point was anything but harmonious. He really tried to break her, and because of who she was and where she came from, he never did. True to form, one month later she graduated Norfolk State and moved to Maryland, pursuing a teaching career and an entirely different kind of light-skinned African-American male with a million dollar smile. Fortunately, after all this time, I think she's finally understanding her worth.

In accepting that my mother and sister have the worst love lives on the planet, I've come to the conclusion that it must be genetic. It has to be. It's an unproven and entirely untestable theory, but for whatever reason, I feel that because my mother and sister had repugnant love lives, I'm destined for romantic disaster. I know this is insane, unfounded, delirious, and doesn't make any sense, but ultimately, I don't want to marry my father. I don't want to reflect on my love life and only see mistakes, accidents, and what shouldn't have been. I want to be stronger than that. I want to not need someone to make me complete. Because as my mother taught me, once you allow that to happen, you choose to release your power, and somehow, someone skillful enough to deceive you may choose to diminish you with whatever you have chosen to relinquish. That's what love does to my family. It destroys us. Love for us is basically every bad Lifetime movie ever made.

There is a saving grace; I know it isn't genetic and there are miracles every day. Couples who choose to be together and continuously love each other with faith and respect are rare, and I have never met a couple fitting those standards until I met my friend Karen's parents. They have been together since they were fifteen, and they still love each other. They treat each other with respect and look at each other endearingly. Naturally, they're foreign—Filipino to be exact. I've become so enamored with this couple's success, I tell everyone about their love. I can't express enough joy that there are still people who marry and love one another, and live happily ever after. Or, at least *ever after*. Many people think I'm giving the synopsis of a Danielle Steel novel because there is a distinct gleefulness that encompasses me when I relay their story. I know I don't know everything about their lives, I know they do love each other.

People, my family and friends, pretty much everyone I share their story with, are quick to remind me that anything could be happening behind closed doors and that I shouldn't think their life is perfect because it appears so through a window. I *know* their lives aren't perfect. I *know* that anything could be happening and they must've really tackled some seemingly insurmountable quandaries over the past twenty years. Just the same, when he looks into her eyes, *I* feel their love and that's something *I've* never experienced. It's not jealousy. It's not envy—okay, maybe a little bit—I consider it admiration. In its purest form, it's aspiration. For the first time in my life, there was a relationship I could aspire to have sometime in the future. A relationship, not to conceit, but worthy of me and all I have to give, and all that I am. It's not that I decided years ago I was never going to find a love like that; it's just initially, watching him watch her, I had begun to believe it was possible.

To declare you are worthy of love is harder for some than it is for others. Every now and then, I feel like I'm the worst person in the world and I don't deserve a second glance from anyone remotely human, but I can say that I do. Relationships are founded on more than personal reservations. Since I'm currently working toward overcoming irrational fears genetically forced upon me by my mother (I can asshole-ishly blame her for anything, really), I think I'm due for a love adventure. Sometime soon, I hope. Small towns aren't the ideal setting for gay love stories; then again, they aren't exactly the ideal location for black men who can impersonate Whitney Houston and Tina Turner (which I've done more than once, thank you!), so I think I can make do for now. Who knows where I'll be in the future? The only thing to do is remember that my mother and sister have their own stories and mine does not have to follow a similar plot. Mine, God willing, could be the extremely rare, affectionate saga that plays on your heartstrings and fucks with your emotions but is ultimately triumphant and moving. Some story in which you can see Katherine Heigl portraying the lead role. I just have to recall how Mr. Anghel looks at Sofia, and remind myself it is possible. And so, permitting myself to believe in love, I can firmly state I believe in life after it, also.

Which brings me back to Cher. I feel that with an affirmative yes I can finally shut the fuck up and go back to dancing whenever the song's playing on the radio or plays on shuffle. After all, I do believe that is the original purpose of an eternal anthem, motivating all to move rhythmically to a classic beat. I don't know where I'd be if Cher hadn't asked me that question. I'm 1000 percent correct when I say there is quite possibly no love story waiting for me, but why not bet against all odds when Cher's in your corner, pushing you to believe just a little more?

Three: IFLYSM

Friendships are good, right? I mean, they're prosperous, long, and supposedly last forever. Eventually you begin to see yourself through your best friends' eyes and can't imagine life without them. That's how it's supposed to go, yes? Always wanting the best for them and wishing them well, being present when they need you, answering when they call, reminiscing in between lengthy periods of visiting one another, being the constant that continually makes their lives better because you genuinely yearn for their success....

This is what friendship truly is and how it's to be executed in its full, illumination. Friendship, and the mere act of being a friend, provides great comfort and nourishment to one's soul. True confidants love each other with the wholeness of their hearts, considering the other person's happiness above their own. Or, as some relationships unintentionally impact lives, leaves half the friendship bond bitter as hell.

That one might just be me.

As any reasonable disclaimer should begin, I officially pronounce my love for my best friend. Tyler Paulson is everything I'm not, and should desire to be. He's optimistic, kind, loving to anyone in his presence, is certain of who he is, and more importantly, who he loves. I know I am a better human being because I'm able to hold him so close to my heart. It's pertinent that I express my love in its depth now—this isn't about how much I enjoy my friendship or my love for him, it's about a disgusting reality; I secretly want him to fail.

We used to spend hours on his couch talking about men, women, and oddly enough, feet. We'd discuss our futures and imagine our ideal lives as the night grew darker and discussions turned more personal. Tyler, always the dreamer, wanted to marry whomever he was dating at the time, always sure he'd found his soul mate in his flame of the week. Craving nothing more than love and sustenance, his desideration was admirable and irrefutably romantic, even if I couldn't stop cringing whenever he'd reference *The Notebook*. Perhaps I was uncomfortable with any references he'd make to his life resembling a Nicholas Sparks novel because I felt like I'd be the one dying of cancer and ending up alone, and that's a fate I haven't any want for.

In contrast, I viewed my future as pragmatically as I could. Focusing on a writing career in some sense of the term, I wouldn't permit myself the slightest desire or need of a love life. Relationships with other people cannot be predicted, and decidedly I for damn sure was not going to factor in the wants and desires of someone else when it came to my future. I planned to leave Virginia and never look back. My goal was to be successful, work hard, and take chances toward prosperity. Then, maybe I could pursue a love life after I arrive wherever I chose to be in life. Virginia was too small for me. I planned to escape any way I found possible. After considerable years of success and commensurate wealth, I would adopt a little girl because I honestly wouldn't have the slightest clue how to raise a son, especially not alone. My life was planned and calculated and everything it should've been. Everything life is not, in reality.

Well, life happened and Tyler moved away, and we never spent time on that couch again. We embarked on separate lives, seldom communicating since people are busy or they soon take on responsibilities they didn't have before. Seeing him once a year became a privilege not lost on me. I focused on my future, and supposedly ironclad plan. Working in overdrive, missing nearly every lunch period of my senior year, I had to try to make my future work. I had to secure a life for myself away from that small town, because with every day and every hour, I belonged less and less to Farmville, and I was determined to force my way out. In that time from August 2011 till December 2011, I was accepted into seven universities, and couldn't afford any of them. I applied for government loans so frequently to no avail; it felt like Obama personally sent me a fuck-you in the mail. Whatever. I wasn't able to college how I wanted, blah blah blah. That isn't important anymore. The door closed on me while I was on my way out. Everyone else got to get on their planes out of there and I was stuck with an invalid ticket, and it was *my* fault. No college. No university. No out. Fuck *me*. Then I viewed not attending college as the greatest personal failure I've ever had to endure.

Meanwhile, Tyler fell in love all over the place. Whenever I would speak to him, it was all about Taylor, or Kenya, or Kayla, Amethyst,

Magic, Jasmine, LaQuisha, Tammy-Lynn, and other colorful names that all required his attention.

Tyler Paulson describes himself by who he's with, at least he used to when we were all dreamers. He once told me, "we are nothing without love" and, "it makes me not want to die." While I still fail to understand the effect another person can have over another, I respect that this is how he strongly feels concerning matters of love. I'm jealous of his susceptibility of affection, I'm in no denial that I'm definitely lacking the necessary skill and natural ability in that department. Repeatedly, he found love in person, over the Internet, and probably with every other girl who suited his fancy. I'm not trying to allege anything here, but he is Tyler Lawleen Paulson. He and love definitely used to be a thing.

Among all the women in the universe, there was one girl who outbitched the others, winning poor little Tyler's heart. He decided to attend San Francisco State University in California to build a stronger relationship with his cyber love. It was that easy for him. Tyler hadn't met Andrea in person; the entire genesis of their relationship existed online and through their Blackberries. My naïveté led me to think an internet-based affair would be drama free—not quite. They argued and fought, everything other couples do, only they did it across the United States of America without ever meeting. That's dedication. Hell hath no fury like Tyler's black, fearless girlfriend. At eighteen and seventeen, they chose to love each other. When Tyler arrived in San Francisco, his girlfriend enveloped him with open arms, and so began their lives together.

Lounging around my home as I routinely checked Facebook, my stomach instantly tightened, invoking sickness and physical despair upon seeing their physical embrace. As I read Tyler had departed Virginia and arrived in California, thunderclouds formed and stormed ferociously over my being. This was uncommon for me. Acrimony has never run parallel in relation to a friend's joviality. Even after I was unable to attend any university of my original choosing (Emerson would've meant the auction of vital organs / body parts. Considered hawking a kidney, drew the line at telling my nuts which one I loved more and which one was tuition), I remained delighted and cheerful about my friend's accomplishments. Normally, I'm genuinely thrilled and support my friends in their endeavors, so this was completely unexpected and new to me; I felt terrible. I have many friends, one best friend, and I couldn't bring myself to offer the proper congratulations. Forthwith, like a good envious Christian, I dropped to my knees and prayed for his prosperity and happiness. I may jocularly remark of how I've become a revolting, nasty demon... that crossed a line even for me. If I can't be happy for my best friend, then clearly I don't deserve happiness for myself.

I think one of the many reasons I couldn't bring myself to glorify Tyler's arrival in all things gay (San Francisco), originated from the first picture he uploaded, smiling in an eatery. He was holding his girlfriend in his arms. In an expeditious fashion, I mentally traveled back two years ago and found myself perched on his couch, massaging his teacup feet. We were partaking in a conversation we've had a thousand times, comfortably waiting for his mother to serve us some kind of ridiculous folksy spread we had both become accustomed to. I couldn't help recalling one of his lasting, overly dramatic pontifications of love and love everlasting. How he'd fight and die for love, and how nothing else was of any meaning. I've come to realize he's finding that now, and I've begun to fathom why I'm mad as hell.

It isn't just his dream coming true, it's mine. I'm the one who wanted to get out and start a new life for myself, and he was the one who was supposed to have all the love. I was comfortable with that. I would've pleaded for that, but now his dream comes true and mine goes to shit. I've worked for everything; I've worked to get out. He just fell in love. I know I resigned myself years ago to surviving on forthcoming independence and success. I know I did it to myself, but he didn't have to take my dream, too. He didn't have to leave me here alone with no way to get out, when that was the only thing I've ever wanted to do. The only thing I dreamed and prayed about for myself, and somehow he got to take it all. Now I think if I never sat on his couch, the winner wouldn't have taken it all... and then again, I know there's no foundation for that to be true. He'd still be in California and I'd still be here, alone.

He was—is—my best friend. I've loved him more than I loved most people, I know that. I never fell *in* love so I never gave someone everything, but if there's one person I gave it most to, it'd be Tyler. He was my closest friend, and like the day he moved, this is the end of an era. Once a year turns into once in every five years, and soon enough that'll be more like once in a decade, or once ever. There aren't any more hugs or creepy-ass foot massages or hearing him call me "Delly." It's simultaneously the death of a friendship and the death of a dream, both of which are leaving me destitute in the rawest sense of the word. There isn't even anyone left to help me pick up the pieces. Their dreams all came true. There isn't any boyfriend to speak of. I've always been the one in opposition to having one. Again, the only thing that seems to remain constant is that I am the main contributor to my own failure. I realize that I'll probably handle and come to terms with this like I do most everything, in solitude.

The only rectitude I can use to justify my unbecoming emotions is the 'stranded, island, drowning, only one can be saved' scenario. Without a doubt, if ever we were on a deserted island and I and anyone Tyler has ever dated was drowning, he'd choose the person he can fall in love with, and if the situation was reversed, I'd choose him every time. It's not a character flaw, it isn't even worth inquiring about, it is just who he is. Tyler Paulson is the person who falls in love.

Nearly two years ago, we sat on his couch and fantasized about the lavish ways in which we'd live out our lives together. He decided we needed a poster and since I didn't, and in some cases still don't, like the word no, we embarked on that adventure together.

He wrote *IFLYSM* and I, in my refined and elegant manner, asked, "What the fuck does that even mean? Is that some goddamn homoerotic prayer?"

He laughed. "No. It means 'I fucking love you so much,' dick head."

Smiling at the sentiment, I made a suggestion: "It looks like a word. Why don't we make it one? Iflysm."

In agreement, he responded, "Our own special word, just for us."

And if he uses it on one of his girlfriends, I'll fucking kill him. My idea of my future and personal fears of our dwindling friendship is something I have to let go, I wish Tyler Paulson the best future anyone can imagine. No one deserves it more. Even if the last time I'll ever see him was that brief moment in April when he came back to visit Farmville, I cherish what time we did have. There are memories, there was the couch, and then there are our own special little words. If this is officially it, I'm glad for at least a brief moment I'd gotten to use words like iflysm.

Four: God Said, "Fuck 'Em!"

Happy people annoy me. Jubilation is pre-career suicide for any artist. We have to suffer; what else are we going to painstakingly display for your consumption? What self-respecting artist acknowledges blatant euphoria, let alone has the audacity to publicly express internal satisfaction? This is a new one. I'm somewhat familiar with contentment—not necessarily possessing the nerve to explore the emotion.

As I stated, happy people tend to be annoying. They are resiliently joyous, lacking reason or depth. I _loathe_ having a bad day, then interacting with someone who cannot stop smiling, even after discovering they've contracted an STD—it's partly why my tenth-choice liberal arts college has been such a drain on me. Sorority girls and frat boys shouldn't be so ecstatic after discovering they've circulated oral syphilis amongst themselves. The experience of joy was a foreign concept for this homo, and often times I remain unsure how to accept it. I mean, I am a queen called bitch.

There are brief moments when I can't ignore it, times when I laugh like an idiot or cry like a six-year-old girl watching the ending of _Frozen_. Happiness could be the equivalent of slitting my artistic wrists, but I will say I recognize the feeling, and I'm not arrogant enough to say my gaiety is warranted. The only absolute I'm sure of is when you feel it, you _feel_ it. Yep, there goes my only chance at ever winning an Emmy. Now I'll never meet Shonda Rhimes.

My family never had issues with happiness. Both of my parents suggested that was all I was ever supposed to be. I just didn't feel it. I don't like reflecting on negative past events; they're all trials and tribulations I've worked through and feel I've sufficiently survived up to this point. On the other hand, I am the one who decided to engage in self-reflection as a means of understanding why I'm bitter and who I really am. I can't say that I remember everything; I remember more of how I felt during past events in my life. I'll try not to draw anything out or be entirely too dramatic, while being as honest as I can. I'm gay, we have a thing about facts and skipping the bullshit.

You've heard the story: gay kid, embarrassingly effeminate, and I thought I was the straightest kid ever. I wanted to be tough, but weighed considerably less than others. I wanted to be big but was incredibly tiny. I wished to be tall, but I was always a foot behind, and I wanted to fit in, but I was gay.

Needless to say, my childhood made for a very uninteresting one. I didn't have many friends, and everyone made fun of me. The only peace I found was watching Whitney Houston in *Cinderella*. Starting in the third grade, it really began affecting me. Since I moved for the first time from my home in Halifax, Virginia, I was with different people in a different small town that was predominantly African-American. Halifax was predominantly African-American, but they were mostly family members who knew and loved me to begin with. Since we attended school in one of the smaller towns, elementary, middle, and high school students rode the same bus. I mean, can you say Bumfuck, Virginia? Diamond (fifteen) attended the high school, Amethyst (eleven) attended middle, and I (eight) elementary school. For the most part, we all looked out for each other and I suppose I felt protected. It helped that Cumberland was a population of about six people and a turtle. Naturally, every red-blooded boy in high school wanted to sleep with Diamond, who'd long since blossomed at about the age of twelve or so. By default, they knew not to fuck with me.

One day I guess she had a really bad case of PMS and stayed home to eat chocolate cake and cry because she didn't go to school that day, and I was vulnerable. I can't remember what they called me; I don't really know what they said at all because it wasn't important. I remember running off the bus crying. They hurt me. My mother saw me crying, having taken off that day to look after Diamond, and called the bullys' parents. Not sure how productive that was given that most of the offenders were close to eighteen. Diamond came back to school the next day and laid down the law, or whatever popular teenage girls do to snotty-ass teenage boys. After my sister's act of heroism, I dried my eyes on the cloak of protection she engulfed me in, having less to anxiously cry about day-to-day. Not that as a third grader I didn't enjoy crying every now and then. It was probably more related to heavy *Lizzie McGuire* episodes than any bullying.

That was the first time words ever really hurt me. A year later, I moved to Chesterfield, a predominantly Caucasian environment, and people accepted who I was, mostly. I even think my fifth grade teacher Mr. Wrigg was gay. He took really good care of me, making sure we fifth graders were treated fair and equally.

Moving back to Cumberland after a year and a half of Chesterfield, things were different. I had remained there for two full years and I believe I grew into my surroundings. I made fun of myself before anyone else could. If you can't beat them, join them, right? I'd mock myself every day, opening myself up for personal ridicule because hey, fitting in is *so* worth it. I berated myself for other people. I'd say I regretted it, but it kept the tears away.

I moved in with my father at the start of seventh grade. Any acknowledgement of his past transgressions has been glaringly ignored by everyone who knew of the circumstance, especially by anyone of blood relation to either the victim or assailant. Again, I relocated to a predominantly African-American area and they literally isolated me. We were required to sit in groups during history; I always chose a corner alone. When our desks were forced to face each other, I always turned mine away to face the wall instead of someone else. They'd mock me for any reason: my teeth (the overbite and gap), my clothes (despite that it was a school uniform) and I didn't get why. I figured it would be hard to mock someone you couldn't ever see. Still, they found a way.

At lunch, out of sympathy I was granted the privilege to sit at a table of about six kids, and believe me, they let me know it. It wasn't until I began sitting alone that others followed. My table of one grew into a table of six, and I couldn't help feeling like the head misfit at the reject table; I loved every minute of it. It turns out I wasn't the only one who didn't quite fit the status quo. Apparently, I was the only one too odd to fake it like everyone else could, which is why I chose to step out and do something my peers wouldn't.

The same year, I encountered a girl named Tiffany. During PE we would always work together and chitchat. I thought we had some kind of relationship as pleasant acquaintances making the day go by quicker. One day someone came up to us, "Why do you associate yourself with him?"

Rolling her eyes, "He won't leave me alone." I wasn't hurt, and I took the hint. Little did they know, I was the only one who really talked to her and she would secretly beg me to be her friend when no one was looking. Imagine my surprise when she had no one to run to as she was booed off the stage during one of our seventh grade award ceremonies. I would've been there for her, but she couldn't be seen with me, and I let her run off stage alone. Nothing she said would've mattered if I had the courage to stand up on my own and clap for her, but alas, I was weak and scared. I don't know Tiffany anymore. It's been five years since that incident and I hope she's doing well now.

Another year and I left my father and Newport News behind, and paid my proper respects to the misfit table I cofounded. I moved back in with my mother, stepfather, and Amethyst in the eighth grade, to the other side of Bumfuck Virginia adjacent to Cumberland. Diamond left for college. I was there for a month when my mother left my stepdad and we moved to Chester, and again I was thriving in a predominantly Caucasian environment. There, many of my peers even assumed I was gay but did not negatively judge me for it. I was asked out by a girl on a Friday, Victoria... I never learned her last name. She was sweet and asked me to be her boyfriend on a note card because I made her laugh. True to form, I went home and talked it over with family members, like every thirteen-year-old boy thinks to do, and on Monday returned with an affirmative yes. Comfortable in that space, most people were treated with kindness and understanding, and the students were actually required to learn. Bullying occurred, only I avoided it. There, I was introduced to learning methods Prince Edward school district didn't use until high school. Thriving in school, two days after accepting Victoria's love request, my mother informed me we were moving back to Prince Edward, having reconciled with Herbert. I never got to see where things would've gone with Victoria, but I think it worked out better for her in the long run. Leaving my only girlfriend became yet another thing I could justify blaming my mother for.

Back at Prince Edward, unknowingly for good, I was heavily ridiculed, referred to as "Gay Lord" often. Being thirteen and in eighth grade, I failed to understand how magnificent that title was, only recognizing the discontent and hatred behind it. I never cried; those days were behind me. There was no berating myself at the amusement of others; I held it in. Externally, I was quiet and gay. Internally, I was fucked. I watched *High School Musical 2* repeatedly that year, and to this day, I don't know why it did, but it brought me happiness and was one of the only things that made me smile during that time. One day Amethyst wanted to watch something else on TV. I begged her to let me watch *High School Musical 2,* for the fifth time. I cited stress-related reasons when she asked me why I had to see it. Then she said something I will never forget.

"What stress do you have? All you have to do is be thirteen and in the eighth grade." And then the little gay bitch fire inside me ignited.

I fired back, "You don't know what I have to deal with everyday. Everyone hates me and I don't know why!" Tears streamed down my face. I was unaware *High School Musical 2* became my salvation. It released fears, anger, doubt, confusion, and any other emotion I refused to allow. Amethyst tried denying me of that, and I couldn't stop myself from grabbing a knife and jabbing it into her throat until she lay lifeless on the blood-stained carpet.

Fortunately, it didn't get that violent. No knives or blood was involved. I did endure a severe catharsis that day, though. I ran into my room, cried for several hours, and for the life of me couldn't realize why I was trying to conform to the ideals of people who disapproved of me. I knew I was better than that. God knew I was better than that, and if I couldn't live my life for myself, I had to live the way God wanted me to. Anything had to be better than accepting the wretchedness I committed myself to. I don't know what it was. There was no need to tote around bibles or dress like a Quaker. God made me who I am. I should love who I am. People were going to hate me regardless. If they were going to hate me for who I wasn't, they might as well hate me for who I am, because I am a beautiful person. No exaggeration. God said, "Fuck 'em."

I began accepting who I am in ninth grade. I met my best friend, my other close friends, joined the drama team, and I became better. I became me. I didn't cry about being hated. I began appreciating life for the most part. Shockingly, remaining in Prince Edward my entire high school career, I don't want to say I came into my own, because I don't know what it means and I don't think I'm there yet, but I got a little closer.

Through the help of one of my peers, Carol, she and I performed in the local university's theater department and gained a rapport with some of the theater students. I was delightfully surprised by how normal I felt there, again a predominantly Caucasian environment. I mention races because I'm accepted primarily in Caucasian environs. It's not that

I don't want to be around people of the same race as myself; it's that for an epoch it felt like they largely didn't want to be around me. I love my color and my culture. Every single white kid didn't love me either, don't get me wrong; at Prince Edward and Newport News plenty had a profound distaste for Princess WaWa. Nevertheless, at Longwood I've met two of the best people I've ever encountered backstage during our production of *Grapes of Wrath,* powdering dirt on our faces. Well, for me it was ash; there wasn't any fake dirt dark enough to noticeably appear on my skin.

Rumor has it, as Derek Island, a blue-eyed blond college freshman, entered the dressing room to change, I remarked, "Dirt never looked so good." He glanced in my direction wordless, astonished.

Here's an issue I find with myself as a person. I never met him before, and here I was making a nonchalant sexual remark to a random Aryan three years my senior. Carol's mother told me she heard about it one day as she drove us to practice, which is why I assumed sooner or later I was going to be served papers and escorted off the campus, publicly banned for life. I'd be forever known as the guy who got banned from a school named Longwood for a sexual remark. There would be years of easily accessible snide remarks. When I went to apologize, Derek said, "Don't sweat it, I'm closeted af." since he's closeted anyway. Well, actually he said he's "no homophobe," but was closeted just the same.

When Derek started reading my Facebook statuses, our friendship really began. His message read, *You have some really cool thoughts and I'd love to text you sometime.* He gave me his number. I can't say I've ever had a crush on him, but I can't say I never have, either. There's a charm to Dare Island. We spent Christmas together via text message. I know his heart; it's pure and just as beautiful as his diamond blue eyes. I love him.

I never knew how much I did him until Whitney Houston died and it felt like I was going to stop breathing. In all my moving and changing schools, she had been with me ever since Halifax. I championed her comeback and prayed for it to last. Sadly, it didn't. No one else really understood or got my depression or incessant mourning like Dare did.

That same year, I didn't get money to attend Emerson like I planned, either, thus entering into a stupor of self-hatred. It was a hard burden, one for which there was no solution. A melancholy misfortune rained upon me, and I wasn't shy about shouting profanities at the forecast. I was cruising Facebook on my cell phone one night and I saw one of Dare's many statuses referencing Whitney's last single, "I Look to You." Trying to remember how long it'd been since I heard the song, I looked it up on my phone and reviewed the lyrics as if I was listening to her with fresh tears. Whatever the lyrics might be: trite, preachy, whatever word or judgment a person would like to place on that moment—I did what I must do. Fighting a losing battle, I laid down my burdens with Jesus. God only knows what it took for me to let that go—life has only taught me how to hold on to things, the things that hurt me.

On my eighteenth birthday, I watched *Seasons of Love* from *Rent* as the clock struck twelve, and I couldn't stop myself from crying, thanks to him. Another person was responsible for my tears. It wasn't because I was inadequate or because they made me hate myself, it was because they loved me and that was something new to me. I've conditioned myself for hate and I know perfectly how to handle it, but accepting love was an overwhelming venture. I was afraid I couldn't contain it. The faggot. The Gay Lord. None of it mattered anymore. For the first time ever, love was louder than any discontent I've ever felt. That's more than a gay boy from Halifax, Virginia could ever wish for.

I'm thankful Derek could love me when I couldn't love myself, for being strong when I am weak, and for being Christian when I forget to be. Here I am, delving even deeper into the end of my career before it begins, burying myself farther into the ground with every word and notion of love, happiness, and the healing outlook of that thing called God. I doubt this will be worthy of the bargain section at Walmart. Good thing I'm a nobody anyway. I will say this; after turning my desk around and facing the wall, berating myself for the amusement of others, I cannot just as easily turn away from love, this artistic lethal injection called happiness, as one would think. I don't know if many people know this or if it's Kim Kardashian and me, but after you've measured life otherwise according to the haters, adhering to *Rent*'s demands by measuring your life in love *is* freedom. I just hope Kim doesn't make any more reality shows, at this rate, she'll be inaugurated in 2024.

Five: The God One

I found God within myself, and I loved her fiercely.
– Ntozake Shange

First and foremost, I would like to apologize if there are excessive references to popular culture throughout this chapter. Pop culture has always been a part of my life, and while it doesn't define who I am, at times it certainly articulates what I am trying to say better than I ever could.

I found myself procrastinating writing this. I think I knew what it would require me to do, something I've never so much as attempted to do before: define what God means to me and what He or She has been to my life. I've always looked at my spiritual relationship as personal, shrugging off questions about Christianity or personal faith. It's gotten to the point I don't know what to call It because I feel it's so unique to me. What I believe works for me, and it is true for who I am, which is why I believe in it. I don't think anyone distanced from my realm of thinking would understand my faith, at least apart from my heart. The idea of God has never been presented to me in a way I felt represented my beliefs. It must only be me who feels a specific connection, right? I'm guessing as I'm hoping I'm wrong. I wouldn't have an issue with having a completely uncommon relationship with Christ; I am curious as to how crazy I really am.

Dating back to as early as I can remember, when I was merely three or four, I felt God in me. No, not in any creepy child molester way—God was in my *soul*. I lack the vocabulary to define anything, because I've gone so long with the justification that I don't have to. God, the Lord, Christ, all dwelled within, and I was a part of that and a part of them. I even feel that today. I feel God lives in all of us; the core of us individually owns a piece of God that makes us who we are.

When I was four years old, I prayed every night and throughout the day continually, trusting and loving the only thing that never disappointed me. My actions may have been mainly the result of a promise. Imagine a lower middle class African-American kid living in the rural south with dreams, gigantic dreams of success and stardom all because the Lord said it was going to happen. I don't have any idea why, internally, I've always had the inclination I was destined for something. It displeases me to sound immodest or arrogant, but I felt I was always predestined for greatness. Most people would know my name, and I was to share my love, honesty, and faith with the world. I don't know what other four-year-olds were doing with their time, but I spent most of mine dreaming about God's prophecy of fame and prosperity. Now I kind of think that was me really just wishing to be Whitney Houston.

This is by far the most outrageous thing I've ever admitted to. I watched *Cinderella* on television one too many times before the tape broke, and I sensed I was supposed to be in Whitney's shoes. I was meant for that kind of success, that kind of love, and that amount of talent. While it's possible that I was attributing my desire to be Whitney Houston to my connection with God, I was *four*. There was a realness there that can't necessarily be explained. I didn't know how to tie my shoes, but I knew God had major plans for my life and they were going to be larger than I could ever envision. It's only now as I grow that I begin to question the realization. The most bizarre thing, however, is I still believe it was the word of God.

Not knowing when or how it came about, I became separated from Christ. Most of my experiences in school were spent isolated on the playground; there weren't many influences present to tear me away from what I held dearest, my relationship with God. I recall classmates gawking my way in youthful confusion, even laughing as I said grace over lunch every day. I knew God, and God was with me. I knew then I was weak in everything else, but I was strong in Christ, and that's something I was indeed proud of.

I would love to entertain ideas about how it happened in middle school, or after several grandparents died. The change occurred when I hit puberty, or in other words, fell into a big fat tub of gay wickedness and sexual debauchery. It was soul crushing, finding out that God didn't love me anymore. I was thirteen and bound by something I couldn't control or love. God has always been a part of me, but then I realized there was another part of me, too, that I just could not rid myself of. I didn't know how to reconcile the two identities.

I had been going to two churches for two years, one Baptist for youth group on Wednesdays, one Pentecostal for Sunday mornings; I reached a point where I couldn't handle it anymore. It had been two years since puberty and I was fed up with the two disconnected areas of my life. I was at youth group when they openly and warmly informed my impressionable tenth grade self all the ways God hated me and my people specifically (not really, but that's pretty much what it felt like, and this is my damn story). The other church I attended, or Church Number Two as I'll refer to it, was weird as hell but still very loving. They were iffy to say the least when it came to peacocks in the pews, and one Sunday morning, I just couldn't sit through another bullshit service. I'm sure everything was proceeding routinely for them, not so for myself.

Not too sure if it was something the pastor said at Church Number Two, or if it was West at youth group comically blurting, "What? Like, don't be gay?" at Church Number One that fateful day, but all the commentary resonated with me. Know those moments when you can feel the whole room *not* look at you?

I was hearing every voice but God's. I was using everything I could to keep negative, pensive thoughts to myself, turn them around, and manufacture a witty comment packaged with a Farah Fawcett smile. I'm partially ashamed to say I didn't have the denial in me anymore. The next Sunday morning at Church Number Two, I got up from the pew, ran to the bathroom, and cried. With a humanizing weakness I wish I didn't possess, I sent an eight part text message to my best friend Karen and my youth pastor, and waited through deafening sobs until I could find the lighthearted quips and Farah Fawcett smile again, and by the time I was prepared to leave the bathroom, I was in full *Charlie's Angel* mode. I wish I could say that and implement it in a cool way, only there was nothing admirable about it. Fake smiles only get you so far, particularly when you're torn in two about who you really are on the inside.

My youth pastor (I feel like such a dork for saying that, "youth pastor") agreed to have lunch with me; his treat. He really is a great man, and one of the better people I have known in life. I'm grateful for his presence, advice, and that he's genuinely there and cares for me. He also pays for my lobster, so I can't complain. We sat down and had a very honest conversation. I don't know what the hell was wrong with me; I think it must've been all the free food shoved in my face. I began to agree to change myself.

Youth pastor Tom wasn't saying homosexuality is a choice, or even that I was in control of my desires—my guess is he once was a fifteen-year-old boy with hormones as well, that's just a guess—he told me, "You need to change yourself for Christ." I couldn't even argue with him; he was operating under biblical instructions. After taking his money and making him promise to purchase me more food sometime in the near future, he dropped me off back at home with his advice and an inspirational website to ponder. And yes, I was inappropriately attracted to him.

I wish I could say somewhere in there I was the superhuman Waldell I like to pretend I am. The one who taps into the fearless black bitch inside and tells anyone who doesn't accept or like me to "kiss my sassy ass, mother fucker." I have an affinity for large alter egos—Princess WaWa, and all. My personalities are strong, beautifully full-figured people who don't have to take shit from anyone, because they don't deserve or have to. I *wish* I could've been a black bitch somewhere in that conversation, all strong-willed confidence with an appreciation for myself and a love of everything I am, but I wasn't. I hadn't exactly regained my strength from that church bathroom incident, so I lacked in everything I should've been.

No need to recall the website my youth pastor gave me. I remember it was intended to be better than others because it recognized homosexuality existed and there wasn't a cure, the organization was solely dedicated to sexual repression. The slogan might as well have read, "This is who we are naturally so we have to hide that so God can love us. No, God doesn't make mistakes, except with you. When He made you, He fucked that up, so we have to fix it. Damn, Jesus." Only it would've been a little lengthy. I give myself credit for not investing time and energy into that load of ironic crap. I know Tom wouldn't have suggested the site unless he trusted it and felt it would genuinely help, so I didn't hold it against him. Plus free food pretty much cancels out all foul play in my book. Except if he had insulted Reba or something.

Turning from the Internet, I sought solace in more concrete forms of religious foundation. Like in most American households, I found my Holy Bible and turned to the New Testament. I know some Christians like to disregard the Old Testament out of convenience, so I skipped to the New in order to avoid slavery, rape, and concubine rhetoric, when I came across one of the more disturbing verses I have ever read. In 1

Corinthians 14:34, the Bible legislates: "Women should remain silent in the churches. They are not allowed to speak, but must be in submission, as the Law says." I was done. That finished me. I had to take a harsh look at life and wonder what God was, because clearly, for me, God was not the Bible. God wasn't some evil man or woman who hated me or said that while these feelings are natural they're completely wrong. God was someone who loved me and reassured me I was worth life. God loved me ceaselessly, and I was busy missing out on acceptance due to self-imposed hatred, pity, and confusion. I almost let God go because someone else told me He/She wasn't supposed to love me.

I decided to release all of it. None of it was mine, nor did any of it have the right to be. God wasn't this. God wasn't hating myself so others could sleep well at night. God was the strength I found at the misfit table. God was the fact I never stopped dreaming even when I was supposed to. God was that moment of honesty and hope when I watched impossible things happening every day. I had to release the God that was everyone else's. He brought me no joy, no affection, and scarcely any kindness. The God I missed and needed, the presence I yearned for, was the one who told a very little boy he needed to prepare his wings because he's going to fly one day.

In a reflective moment, I read *The Color Purple* in the seventh grade. The scene that remained with me the longest was when Celie told Mr. she was "here." I struggled to completely comprehend that statement until I heard Fantasia sing "I'm Here" at the Tonys via YouTube. Her earnest and uncomparable performance was an example of what it means to be whole in Christ. I wish more people knew. Everyone searches for God outwardly, when the truest form of God resides within. I suppose many won't know that until they have a relationship with Christ and it's gone, but I couldn't afford to not have it anymore.

Accepting God again, I've made my peace with certain ideologies. I no longer need to look to other people for religious approval. I no longer need to be enraged at someone else's blatant ignorance. Now when someone tells me no one's born gay, I don't have to say, "Oh really, mother fucker? You don't know shit. When was the last time you were gay, asshole?" It's not only the ignorance that bothers me, it's certain individual's unwillingness to be wrong. Seriously, some can't even admit the possibility of being incorrect about an experience they've never endured. I waste energy on the thoughts and feelings of others, then I remember this is the United States of America, and it's people's natural born right to remain stupid, including Rush Limbaugh's. I find peace in God, and nothing else matters. I was born with a fairly tight one, so I needn't worry about other assholes.

Living as I do, I admittedly face hardship in explaining this to other people. The answer is long and requires a plethora of time and consideration from both the questioner and the questioned. Trying to simplify it down to one sentence, God is the honest version of myself, connected to all things glorious and true to divinity, including heaven and the earth. That's one of the reasons why I never stick to masculine or feminine pronouns. I know God presents him or herself as masculine in the Bible—take a guess as to which sex authored those books. As a hint, it wasn't the one not allowed to speak in church—for me, God changes depending upon the person. God is always the same, but omnipresence reveals itself in infinite ways. The only way for God to make sense, she has to be present in all of us individually, us being male, female, transgender, etc.?

I am not an authority on religion or theologian. As I previously stated, I don't know shit. I know this is my story and this is what's true for me. God for someone else may be completely different and strictly by the Book and that's okay. I've found the God that's real to me as one should seek. For me, despite alleged abuse of power, I don't think it's *ever* okay to tell someone they cannot speak or ask questions in a church setting according to the "Law." It's an independent stance, and I fully support it. That's not for me, nor is that order of faith one I subscribe to. Celie telling Mr. about himself is God. The mother attending her children's funeral and surviving their death is God. God is that moment when you cannot deny his/her love or strength anymore, and all you can do is accept it. Whether or not I'm a Christian I guess would depend on someone else's opinion of me. I believe in God and I believe Christ died on a cross, but I also believe She loves me in spite of and in conjunction with my homosexuality. Whatever my label is, it's not important to me. I know who I am and I know what I believe. So, to answer the question that so many have asked me over the years, that's who God is to me. And fuck, She's fabulous.

Six: Because of You

My relationship with my mother begins as unclear as the meaning of this entire... *collection?* Maybe our story starts when my father left and a part of her died. Could it have been the day she married my stepfather, in the midst of a terrible storm, at a church she'd attended numerous times with my father before the necessary termination of their marriage? Could it have been she and Wilbert, her most recent husband's, first fight? Their third? When he first exercised his personal child-rearing techniques? Was it Niles, the Englishman she briefly dated after she and my father separated? Could it have been before I was even born? Before any of my sisters were ever conceived? Is it my failure? Is it my existence that would serve as a justification for my mother's alcoholism?

Attempting to state a point of reference in which I can recall knowing my mother, actually *knowing her*, immediately deviated into trying to discover the cause of her alcoholism. My writing this isn't intended to find why my mother often lacks sobriety. The intent is to identify my standing with her as a person, and to dissect the root of my relationship with mother. My main issue is my relationship and her alcoholic history have become inseparable. I may not receive any answers, only glimpses of realizations, but this is the truth of what remains pertaining to myself and my mother.

Everything I have ever said about my mother has either been a lie or some aggrandized hyperbole of the actual truth. My earliest memory of my having to defend my mother's parenting was during sophomore year in 2009. I had attended, as per the request of a friend, a Governor's School recruiting seminar. An invitation was extended to all students and parents who might be interested in the program, having their child finish their senior year with an associate's degree. I didn't plan to attend until I received the direct request on the day of the meeting. In the past, I had always been more independent than most my age. Arriving unaccompanied, I recognized the mother of a friend of mine and either she took a seat next to me or I took a seat next to her. We discussed *My Sister's Keeper* by Jodi Picoult, saying she's read every novel by her. As the conversation progressed, she questioned the presence of my parents. It sort of startled me because since my parents' separation in 1999, I'd grown accustomed to doing things for and by myself.

Somewhat confused and curious about my absent mom's whereabouts, Nirvana asked, "Where are your parents?"

Searching for a reply to the peculiar question, I responded, "Um... at home?"

"Really? Why isn't she here?" she pursued, referring to my mother.

"She's sleeping." I had suspected Mother'd been drinking, given it was past five p.m. Generally, Mother begins indulging rather quickly after returning home from work. I lied to Nirvana, but it was an understandable, respectable lie; normally after Mother drinks, she falls asleep or passes out. Sometimes in bed, or on her bedroom floor, more recently a few times in the kitchen, and I'm assuming that unconsciousness constitutes some form of an energy revitalizing dormancy.

Next, Nirvana continued to push, "She didn't get up to come with you?" I could see the negative conclusions beginning to formulate in her mind.

I knew I couldn't tell the truth. She seemed like the kind of person who would really do something if she thought I needed it, and I was not prepared for my life to change. So, I lied again. Or further embellished. I mean, I did, in a sense, speak the truth.

"She works a lot," was all I could muster. Did I mention that the lady I was speaking with runs a business and owns her own company? *She* managed to put in her appearances regarding the educational welfare of her son.

"I just always thought you had these great parents." I suppose that was a compliment to me in some way; it meant she assumed I was raised well or that I carry myself as if I've had a proper or superior upbringing. I couldn't bring myself to accept it as that. I can't recall whether or not I responded defending my mother.

Most likely I persisted with, "She's tired, but she's a great mom," I can't state I said that as a fact.

I knew the circumstances weren't the best. I truly believed, and to some value still believe, my mother did and does the best she can. I used to feel she was indeed the best mother—I'm not too positive I can support that argument anymore. At the time, however, I could defend her at least to myself. Cognitively, I could rationalize why she did what she did. Why she drank rather than communicate.

My mother's life is hard. Her mother was in a nursing home in her final years, my father by that time, failed to contribute anything to her children's life and health. Mother was the first and last person we all relied on for anything financially; her job is demanding, both physically and intellectually. She works as a nurse in a county jail. My two older sisters were in university, and no matter how independent I claim to be or know I am, I'm always dependent when it comes to necessities. The weight of the world is on my mother's back, so is it acceptable for her medicate her sorrows with the most addictive legal drug in the United States of America and most parts of the world. I'll allow it. From that point until now, she could let it define her without heavy consequences.

I mentioned my friend's mother runs a business; the majestic Nirvana also has a contributing husband. She has a college degree, an upper-middle-class house on the hill, and two sons who hardly ever want for anything. Working may not have been a sufficient excuse for my mother failing to appear or involve herself more in my academic career, but it was sufficient for me. I didn't invite her because her life is, at times, agonizing. I didn't invite her because I was going to have to learn how to rely on myself. I knew she probably would have been there for me if I told her in advance or made a show of how I needed her to be there, but seeing her spread thin and the liquor bottles' proof warnings rising, I chose not to add any more stress than necessary.

My sisters involved her, especially Diamond, and although no one directly asked me to, I willingly trudged through the shortfall. I've been conditioned that way, thinking back to kindergarten and how once my paternal aunt suggested my mother regularly dressed me for school, which never actually happened. Mother would leave the clothes I was to wear laid out in the morning, but I dressed myself whenever I elected to actually go. I stayed home with my ailing grandmother a lot in pre-kindergarten. My mother, of course, was obligated to work. Sometimes, you have to suck it up and make it through by yourself. This, calamitously, is how I've learned to do most things.

The most common way people in my life were introduced to my mother happened in an explosive manner. My mother ultimately became more Facebook famous than I am. The inciting incident occurred when I made a post about a university I was applying to. There were three different kinds of "Mother" statuses I created. There's the directly from my mother status, the inspired by my mother status, and the entirely fictional status.

Example one, directly from my mother: Riding in the car from South Hill to Petersburg

Me: *Mother, when I get married, are you coming to the wedding?*
Mother: *Of course, I expect to be the one who gives you away.*
Diamond: *Brother, we'll all be there. I just hope he'll have enough money to support the rest of your family too.*
Mother: *I'm sure he'll be a lovely white man.*

Sometimes... I love my family! ♥

Example two, inspired by my mother: Riding home from graduation

Me: *So Mother, what are you most proud of?*
Mother: *The fact that after changing schools seven times, you never lost sight of your goal. I'm proud of the fact that you already have your first year and a half of college done. I'm proud you have above a 3.5 GPA, and above all that, I'm most proud of the fact you handled all that and managed to teach me how to properly walk in heels. So, in the words of your beloved idol, 'Here's your one chance, Fancy, don't let me down.' Just don't become a prostitute. You make a very pretty drag queen, though.*

My mother has said these things at one time or another, however not altogether and I've never taught her how to "properly walk in heels." That last proclamation seemed to add style and the little extra flair necessary to make it worthy of my Facebook status status quo. And Mom's ringtone for me is "Fancy" by Reba McEntire.

Example three, entirely fictional: Attempting to ride out my laziness

Mother: *Come help prepare for dinner tomorrow.*
Me: *I'm a man. Men don't cook.*
Mother: *NOW you choose to be a man? Yesterday you wore heels and a That's So Raven sweater. Get your ass into the kitchen.*

...Clearly nothing's changed.

Now the only "mother" status that has survived is the completely truthful one. I think I've matured a tad as far as social media goes.

The reason why I've created a Facebook personality for my mother was accidental. The celebrity of writing something, expecting maybe five people to read it, and suddenly twenty to thirty people are validating the writing online and even more people referencing it, quoting lines to you in person when they see you in the local Walmart the next day was intoxicating. I began and continued a pseudo-series of "mother" statuses. Could my mother be to me as Soph is to Bette Midler? I'm not sure, but my mother was a functioning way to practice material that others seemed to really enjoy.

I made a point to never lie to anyone about any specific status. Oddly enough, I value my friends and family, and luckily up to this point the only statuses that have ever been questioned were either 100 percent true or partially true as I remembered it, only funnier. Maybe they could see through the fictional statuses entirely, which is how I've gotten by without answering for wholly false recounts.

I will admit I became selfish with my Facebook stardom or recognition, or whatever one would categorize that phase of attention seeking. People were remembering my words, appreciating delightful, family oriented anecdotes. In a large way, my statuses have been my first experience connecting with a specific demographic. And honestly, I got off on the notion that in a sense these people were entertained by me.

I'm positive it was the notoriety that appeased me; I also reaped benefits that facilitated a romanticized view of my relationship with my mother. Reading my statuses, one would think I have the best mother and son relationship in the world. Truthfully, I barely speak to my mother. I doubt she likes me as a person. I'm a big personality, and not everyone's going to agree with that. My mother just happens to be one of those people. This doesn't make her bad, and it really isn't her fault. I'm not blaming her for that. The statuses, though, afforded people the reassurance of my phenomenal upbringing. Something I desired so they would stop asking questions I didn't wish to answer. I don't know if this makes me psychotic, pathological, or what have you, but I know I used Facebook to deceive its users and my friends. It's strange, the lengths I would go through instead of confronting realities I excused because they were inexcusable.

I was ten when I first realized my mother was an alcoholic. I remember the exact night in summer 2005. She'd been drinking excessively, clearly inebriated. I never saw it as a sin to see my parents drink. She grew more tired as she drank, and I was ten years old when I saw my mother pass out drunk for the first time. I knew her drinking problem had gradually increased as she fell unconscious. I went to my room to ask God's forgiveness for not having the strength to deal with it. I told my sisters that evening I was going to live with my father next year. I couldn't take it anymore. That was another reason why I went to live with my father, other than the gay thing.

I moved in with him for the 2006/2007 school year and returned to my mother that June. Things had progressively gotten worse. We lost the house my stepfather had had for decades and relocated to a tiny apartment in the center of town. Her passing out was practically nothing by that time. It used to be that my instinct was to help her, but more and more often, it became to step *around* her. She argued with my stepfather nonstop and even engaged in physical altercations with him and my sister. I was never there when the actual physical altercations took place. When I was present, yelling was her primary vice. I didn't think there was much I could do to aid the situation. One time, I did stop my mother when she tried to physically throw Amethyst out of the house, but that was the only time I can actually remember stepping in. They've tried their best to raise us, or maybe they feel it's their right. However, I don't think either one of my parents were involved enough in our lives to earn the right to hit us.

It was one of the hardest things I've ever endured, and something I suppose I forgot as time passed. That was a hard year for Amethyst. She contemplated suicide, or so she told me. I never thought she would actually go through with it. I try to be there for her when I can, when I see something really affects her. I remember often, after arguing with Mother, she'd wish she would die, and she felt mother didn't like her, or love her. Something we've come to realize over the years is that mother does for us out of a sense of duty rather than out of love. That's the demeanor in which she gave to us. Amethyst's probably the person I'm closest to in the world, and since we've moved around constantly, she's been the only constant friend I've had before or since high school. Growing up, we were together so much our names were called simultaneously. Amethyst-Maine[1], a two-for-one deal. To this day, it rattles me when something hurts her deeply.

That's when I became hardened against mother. In one of their arguments, my mother choked my sister. Amethyst left the house and Mother locked the door, which occurred multiple times. That's when I started releasing her, extinguishing the idea of a loving mom who would be everything we needed, because at that specific time in her life, she wasn't. I've said some harsh words against her that I'm not proud of; she's said some harsh words against us. I'm ashamed to say when we were going through the thick of it, watching my sister battling depression in a local church pew after an awful argument with my mother, I might have said something to the effect of "fuck her." Or "she should die." These are the worst statements one could ever think or say about another person, let alone their mother, but my sister's fragile, and Mother knows that. And it's nothing less than she's told me face-to-face before. I can't even recall if I've said that. I know what I did say was terrible. And yet, I would still like to reiterate *how* ashamed I actually am. This was four or five years ago, and failing to recall what I've said, I'm mortified at the chance of ever having said anything remotely similar to that. I know I am everything I am, positive and negative, mainly positive, because of my mother.

When she's inebriated, Mother has a way of talking directly to you, making you feel like shit. Not even cow shit; that's accepted and maybe even glorified in some countries, but pig shit. The kind the pig keeps eating because it's his instinct. Well, even if you don't want to eat your shit anymore, Mother has a way of continually serving it up to you.

"Call your father," she'd instruct us. "You're so ungrateful" was her favorite line. "Yes, die." She said once. These phrases are benign

---

[1] Maine is my childhood nickname.

compared to the effect they have. Coming from your mother in a state of vile, screeching drunkenness, these would wound deeper than Hamlet's hesitation[2]. And just when you think you've swallowed it all, there she comes curbside with another shitty order.

My mother has great burdens in her life and she won't hesitate to inform you you're one of them. More than likely, it's the two of us. Amethyst and I are the worst. We are failures in that we don't rely on our father for anything, mainly because he's rarely ever good for anything. He tries, though more than likely we'll be wasting time and energy relying on him for anything, in her words. If it comes down to it and he is the deciding factor for something we need, at least I know I'll more than likely go without. Disregarding that process entirely, I rely on my mother only when necessary. I've known we were struggling or "poor," as we've incorrectly categorized it, and I never really asked for much, or I would try not to. I would sacrifice field trips, gadgets, and other items other people had because I didn't think it was worth it or that I needed them, which I don't, and never have. I know it's unfair when you have two parents to rely solely on one, but is it fair if you're the product of two parents and one hardly ever-to-*never* contributes their proper share to your life? There's the root of the main conflict. She's paying for our father's sins—trust me, we all have, too. That's what she fails to see. My father's unequal parenting has affected the three of us as well. Or didn't she notice when I couldn't attend any college or university outside the state of Virginia in the fall? I barely qualified for state loans because when I graduated high school in 2012, my father hadn't paid taxes since 2003. It's like she just sees her pain; yes, she has to suffer through her and my father's missteps, but I do as well.

Every time I needed anything, my mom would get drunk and scream about it. She's mean. In many aspects, I began looking at her like a bully from school. She would say things, pretty much anything with the intention to personally afflict. It's not that the words were objectively that hurtful, it was the anger behind them. I learned to internalize the majority of the hurt and disappointment she'd intentionally inflict on me and see her transgressions for what they were: negative manifestations of her grief as her own problems. These were things in her life she needed to deal with and wasn't able to, therefore she began

---

[2] Here's a hint: everyone dies.

projecting them onto me. I can state that with confidence, not to say her insults didn't still inflict pain and negativity.

Interestingly, the one only time I wasn't instinctually objective is when she hurt Amethyst. I know she's fragile and feels things so much more than everyone else, so her being attacked felt terrible. The few times in my adolescence when I have been brave enough to tell someone about my life at home, I've always revealed it in a comical arena. I wouldn't state it casually, only during times it became impossible to ignore. Like times when Ma would call me nonstop and I would be at a friend's house. She'd proceed to scream through the phone, threatening to call the cops if I didn't return home immediately, slurring her words with every breath. That happened several times when I'd hang out with Carol, Karen, and our friend Johnny, or even at youth group. From then on, I would only discuss the truth if I needed an outlet. I didn't feel comfortable discussing my feelings with everyone. Diamond, maybe, but she wouldn't understand; she left before Ma's drinking became too much of a real problem. Amethyst? She'd be too sensitive. For a long time, I chose to forgo, mostly. And I know my sisters would try to make the situation all better, and I knew it wouldn't ever be, not the way they wanted. I just wanted someone to validate my emotions and feelings as real.

I went to therapy once and confided in the one person contractually obligated to remain silent. Conflicting schedules prevented my return to confide any further. I revealed the ordeal to youth pastor Tom during one of our lunch dates.

"I read the chapter on your mother. How have you been dealing with it all?" It was the break after his salad course, before the main dish.

I said, "I get over it."

"I know you do, Waldell. How?"

"No, literally when she passes out, I step over her." And thus far, that has been the extent of my "dealing with it."

She told me to die once, just as I did her. I don't know how it got that far, mother and son wishing or proclaiming death onto one another—somehow we'd made it there all by ourselves—not quite the picture perfect Facebook status, is it?

As peculiar as it may seem, I still love my mother very much, and I believe she is a pretty great mom. She works nearly every day, and I've never gone without any necessity, ever. When it came to my going to university, or graduating high school for that matter, she's always been the only one who's supported me financially. And even beyond that, she is a good mother when you need her to be. In the eighth grade, she accomplished one of my wildest dreams: she took me to a Reba McEntire concert... and in ninth grade, she took me again. Reba and Kelly to be exact, the Two Worlds Two Voices tour. It does not justify everything, or anything. For two nights, everything was perfect, and my mother being there and stepfather navigating the highway were responsible for it. I'll work because she's always worked. I'm currently studying English at Christopher Newport University and am successful because she's enabled me to be. As I've previously stated, I am who I am because of my mother.

It's when she drives drunk that I become agitated or afraid. It's when she becomes belligerent that I retreat within myself and resolve to run away. It's when she makes me wish she had gotten an abortion that I try to distance myself from her and her decisions, feeling her life would be better without any of us, or without me specifically. Two children would've been enough, but three? Not to mention I'm gay and dress like a girl sometimes. She's had a considerable amount of pain, yes, but I never want to go through what she's gone through, and certainly not with the same results. She is a strong person, and I've never seen anyone more beautiful than her on her wedding day, July 27, 2002. That was the day I gave my mother away to my stepfather. Farther down the road in all her strength and beauty, I've never seen someone so mean and weak. And I'm never more disappointed than when she drives drunk, endangering not only herself but others as well. She should know better.

On her way to work one morning, she flipped her car over on the side of the road. She would've died because supposedly she "saw a deer." She called my stepfather that morning at five a.m. Before anything bad happened, we all knew she was still drunk as she swerved out of the driveway. My stepfather, Amethyst, and I didn't dare try to stop her; it was too early in the morning to strap up for a losing battle. I was on my way to Newport News, preparing to go to my university orientation the next day, when my stepfather passed Mother on the highway, the truck she drove lying flat on the driver's side, trapping her in. Thankfully, there were two kind highway patrolmen there assisting her already, since we couldn't make it there in time. Wilbert stopped the car briefly as we passed, enraged that Mother destroyed his precious 2001 black

Toyota pickup. He was parked on the side of the road, watching the men help my mother, when Amethyst ran out of the car to view Mother trapped in Wilbert's wrecked truck. Amethyst was sobbing uncontrollably and couldn't breathe. When she finally returned to our car, I had to tell her to try to take deep breaths, and reassured her everything was okay, that if Mother was truly knocking on death's door, we'd be the first persons notified.

And I didn't cry. Someone needed to call Diamond and tell her what happened, and I couldn't sound worried on the phone; it only would've agitated the situation. I couldn't fall deep into my emotions; who else would help Amethyst breathe when she thought our mother was going to die? I refused to accept impending doom. Among the three of us, my mother's children, someone had to be okay to calm the nerves and fears of others. I ignored thoughts of what could've happened or what phone call we could've received instead, and focused on what hadn't occurred, even though it scared the shit out of me.

I didn't react until I reached my destination, my father's house. Amethyst and I were staying with him until our respective campuses reopened. I laid down to rest, and woke up again alone with my thoughts. I began confronting the reality of what could have been in solemn misery as Amethyst tossed and turned vigorously asleep in the background, now delighting in the calm and assuredness that morning had stripped her of—the two opposing reactions occurring in one dormant being. I began to listen to Whitney Houston and think of her yet again. She was so young and beautiful when she passed. She has been one of my greatest inspirations of all time, and I loved her dearly. Whitney had an addiction and it was scary and it took her away in the end, and I just don't want my mommy to be like Whitney Houston. I don't want to say goodbye to her and I don't want to hate her or pretend it's okay when she trips over the bathroom toilet and falls asleep in the bathtub. Even if I've thought it once when she'd hurt my sister, or said it when I saw stinging torture in Amethyst's eyes, I really don't want my mother to die. I don't know what I'd do without her.

And through all the pain and the hurt, fear and tears, I don't feel "shaken up" as Diamond once phrased it over the phone. I'm not encompassed by anger, and though I'm afraid of what will happen one day, as with Whitney and her substance abuse, I'm not living in fear. I've been strong for entirely too long. Depended upon by my mother, or

Amethyst when she needs me, I'm tired of being the one with strength, offering a lack of emotion or none altogether to be the one who has no pain when tensions are running high. Who is ever going to be strong enough for me? I'm done with leaning on myself and eating my emotions, choking back the shit Mother serves me like it's Ovaltine and good for my system. That doesn't mean I don't care. It means I will express it to those I can and choose to rely upon, those who have been my support base since I could recall. While I'm a strong and largely independent person, I need someone for me. I need strength from someone other than myself; self-sufficiency can get you but so far. Not anymore. There's only so much strength one can restore by themselves.

During college orientation, I was amongst transfer students, the average age being roughly twenty, though I was eighteen. Parents were invited. I didn't feel it necessary or expect many parents to attend. Before that day, it didn't occur to me so many twenty-year-olds include their parents in so many facets of their lives. It's not that I didn't have a parent who would come; I didn't ask. A side effect of self-sufficiency. I came in, needing to apply for housing, schedule classes, and finalize financial aid documents. From the look of things, it mainly was the parents insuring the future of their now-grown children. I embraced an odd sense of satisfaction that I had the strength and preparedness to fight and work for myself, and not have to have a parent plan that would secure my every need for me.

Toward the end of orientation, there was a penny collecting ceremony, to redistribute to the school's fountain upon commencement. As I stood on stage looking out in the crowd, it was bittersweet not seeing anyone for me there. I knew it was I who worked to get myself there, with the encouragement and support from a few along the way, and it helped me appreciate how much I've grown and how soon. My mother showing up wouldn't have been intolerable. She did make everything in my life possible, and she was there and didn't turn her back on me when I came out of the closet. And after all, it was her and her alone who paid for my deposit to attend CNU in the first place.

I knew deep down I appreciated that my father wasn't there. It would've felt like he'd been majorly contributing to my success, and that's just not true. During the accident, I thought that my mother couldn't die because then we'd be left with our father, and that just would not be fair. My father isn't a bad man. He has in the past put his girlfriend over his children, something I credit my mother with never having done. I love my father with all my heart, and life sort of kicked his ass as well (and he's deserved it), but right now this isn't about him.

In no way am I ever saying I'm the perfect child. Often times, I haven't any idea what to say or how I'm sounding when I say it. I'm inappropriate and direct, and plenty of times, I say exactly how I'm feeling. I don't always have the nicest feelings. How could I ever be perfect when I've said the most disgusting things one could ever say about anyone, and I directed it toward my own mother? I know I could not fully express the relationship between my mother and me unless I was entirely honest. We've both had our darkest moments and said the worst and most hurtful words we could think of to one another or about one another. My mother isn't a monster. She isn't a mean ugly snake that's going to strike inconspicuously. My mother is a woman with a drinking problem that has colored most of my life. She is sound and she is human, and when she is sober, she is perfect.

I wish I could take back the nasty things I've said, or have thought. I wish my relationship with my mother could have been different, will be different, or that she could've had a better life. I wish I didn't grow up so quickly, or as cold as I have. And I hope, one day, our relationship will improve. I'm thankful for the relief in realizing that I can't do it on my own, and that I'm not supposed to.

The greatest nights of my life was when my mother took me to see Reba and Kelly at the Norfolk Scope Arena in January 2008. It was wonderful; it was exactly what I wanted and what I *needed*. Remember, middle school wasn't the greatest experience for me. "Up to the Mountain" is a song they performed, inspired by Martin Luther King's prophetic final speech. It makes me think about how my mother works, and the sacrifices she's been the only one in my life to make for me so I could have the opportunities that I do. I'm thankful for all of them. I know there have been many. There is a song, though, that is so accurate it's frightening. "Because of You" written by Kelly Clarkson when she was sixteen, about issues she had with *her* mother. We look to our parents to be perfect, when they're just as broken as the rest of us, and we have the audacity to hold it against them.

I'm not blaming my mother for everything that went wrong in my life. She's responsible for most of the good as well. I can't deny the effects alcoholism has had on my life. It forced me to be strong and hide my fear. It also made me *expect* her to be in a car accident one day. If there is one thing to take from this, I want to reassure myself that I love my mother, and I am not to take her for granted, and most importantly, I am not imposing her life onto my own.

There comes a point when all must accept reality as it happens. The good, the bad, the ugly, and the Reba McEntire songs. I shouldn't have waited until a car flipped on the interstate to be honest with Mother and myself. Time becomes incredibly short and its speediness and repetitiousness become dangerously realistic. Mother always asks me what I'm going to do if she dies and isn't here to provide for me anymore. My best guess is, I'll survive. It'll be the worst day of my life, and I'll regret every negative thing I've ever thought or said even more than I do now, but I am positive no matter how much I'm angry with life, when and if that unfortunate day should ever pass, I'll put my shoes on one foot at a time and walk on. There is nothing satisfying or glamorous in surviving the day of someone's death, and although I can think of nothing less preferable, I will. In many ways, I am my mother's son. I'm a survivor, by nature (& nurture). That is one thing, from this day on, I will never be ashamed to admit. My mother taught me how to walk on, and so I will always carry her with me.

Seven: Loss Times Two

My father's girlfriend is dying of cancer, and she isn't my favorite person in the world. I find myself at odds emotionally with the situation. People don't just start liking people because they're dying, do they? They're still the same person they've always been. Why should a terminal illness alter someone's perspective of somebody else if not a damn thing's changed about the person, only they're dying? Well, because assholes who don't have a random change of heart for the deathly ill burn in Hell, directly under the overwhelmingly malodorous aroma of Satan's scrotum, for all eternity, right next to Hitler... and for *some reason*, I doubt Hitler'd prefer a seat next to the likes of me. So, I'll reevaluate the basis of our relationship—my father's girlfriend and I, not me and Hitler—and attempt to focus on what good there was/is, even if it was rare. I really don't think I'd like the stench of Satan's balls.

Following my parents' divorce, I reached a level of maturity that prepared me for whomever my parents brought home, despite the circumstances; whether their partners were married, divorced, separated, kind, emotional, delusional, clingy, patronizing, self-deprecating, mentally unstable, wealthy, poor, sick, jobless, condescending, or financially dependent, I got comfortable separating myself from my parents' romances, having long since relinquished the idea of having a big happy family. Their partners desired my parents individually, not necessarily with their brood in tow.

When I met Wendy Fish, it was typical, nothing different except for the face and name, and she appeared to make my father happy. There's really not much more a child can wish for regarding their aging single parents. I encouraged their relationship with my full blessing. I mean, at least my father had upgraded from his usual tastes and met a woman with a job and some form of financial security.

Genuinely amicable initially, Wendy was never intellectually challenging. I take it she hadn't desired to be; not everyone does. She was clearly overjoyed that she had my father, or more frankly, a man.

One summer I spent with him between my junior and senior year of high school, we would all sit in the living room and watch *So You Think You Can Dance* every Wednesday, and we always had dinner (usually fried chicken) at around seven at night, when my father was sure to be off work. That was when Wendy was still working in the mailroom. I would have their apartment to myself for most of the day. Our relationship benefited from a reasonable distance. I'm not always the easiest person to be around for extended periods of time. She indeed had cancer then and was dealing with it, remaining optimistic. Surprisingly, she was entirely dissimilar from the woman I would soon come to know. Back then, we were all very polite, very casual, and simplistic. This was one of my parents' partners. I felt no desire to know her on a deeper, personal level. It's how I prepared myself for when I'd likely stop seeing her. We spoke when she'd return from work:

"How was work?" I'd ask as she'd plop down on the couch, easing into life across the screen from a *Dr. Phil* episode.

"It was okay. How was your day?" she'd respond.

"Fine. I just watched some TV and cleaned a little bit."

"Oh, thank you for cleaning." She has a deep voice, and always uses her manners as I presume she'd been taught by her parents during her youth in the seventies. It is cordial and authentic in a non-demanding way. I had been cognizant of the issues she'd been having with my Amethyst. She and Wendy would be in a room together not saying anything, as a result of neither one of them knowing how to speak first. Well, scratch that, I think Amethyst never had the intent to. She's said on multiple occasions that if Wendy would like a relationship with her, she would talk to her if Wendy spoke first. It's Wendy who wants the relationship, and Amethyst who can perfectly survive without it. It's trivial bullshit, but they let it eat at their relationship so viciously, they've effectively diminished all capacities for kinship. And there lies the foundation of the eternal Amethyst-Wendy bitch-off. Personally, I think it'd make more sense if they were dueling for my father's love, but by the looks of it, it's an overly dramatic pissing contest... and I wonder if any one of them knows they both have vaginas.

That was one summer, and everything thereafter was different. The next time I stayed with my father was several years later after I graduated high school. Not being able to enroll in Emerson, I refused to become consumed by Farmville, Virginia. By the time my friends were off at university, I called my father and told him I was coming to stay with him for four months. I made sure it was a statement rather than a request on the phone. That was the plan until I was able to transfer to an in-state institution and complete my associate's degree online. Also, I planned to find a job that year. Funny thing, no job ever tried to find me.

Anyhow, the impromptu nature in which I informed my father of his near-future living arrangements proved to be an imposition on Wendy since Amethyst was coming to stay for a short while as well, until she got her campus housing ordeal straight with Virginia State. She was relying on funds expected to come from my father, so I assume she knew she'd be waiting a while for him to come through.

Before we arrived, my father called me, "Hey, do me a favor. Call Wendy and tell her you'll help contribute around the house." They'd moved from the apartment I spent last summer at into a house they rented from relatives. I agreed, feeling the method of interaction was somewhat peculiar. If Wendy wanted to ensure I'd clean, why wouldn't she call me directly or instruct me to clean upon arrival? Either way, I called and assured her I'd be a helping hand during my stay. Amethyst warned me of how often Wendy and I'd have indirect conversations; I simply knew in my mind that was how she behaved with my sister because Amethyst was so confrontational. Not axiomatically disrespectful—certainly abrasively direct if the situation calls for it. I was going to be different. I was the friendly one. I'd be caring and easy to speak with, I'm sympathetic and I knew she was sick and I was only going to make life easier for her, or so I thought.

As soon as Amethyst and I arrived, we said greetings, loaded our bags in the back room as neatly as we could, and were off catching the bus to the mall. Amethyst admittedly hated being in the house with Wendy; she had more experience than I did, and left whenever possible. The bus schedules were our salvation. We'd leave as soon as we woke up and come home nearing eight at night. There'd always be people hanging around my father's house, eating, laughing, drinking, and playing Spades. When I asked him why they came so often, he said it's because he likes being around people. It was then I realized my father's more popular than I am, not only going to parties every other night but *being* the party. Which is fitting since he has a higher toleration for loud drunkenness.

During this time, I'd still wake up every day around noon and clean. I'd wash the dishes, sweep the floors, and clear the table; the kitchen left routinely spotless. I'd also clean the bathroom about once a week or as necessary, and similarly with mopping the floors. Even with my compliance to the rules, I'd still get calls from my father while he was at work, instructing me to help Wendy clean, while she was in the house within shouting distance. This was not my preferred method of communication, but I sucked it up because she was ill and I was staying in her home and I didn't want to be rude or an inconvenience. When certain family members of hers would appropriately visit, I'd speak with them after I cleaned or before and after I returned from the mall as I saw fit to do. Amethyst would have to catch buses to Virginia State University most mornings, and while I had classes, I could do them at my leisure, considering they were online to supplement a two-year degree. Generally, Wendy, Amethyst, and I were on friendly terms.

My father has always viewed us as his children. It didn't matter that Amethyst and I were twenty-one and eighteen respectively. He felt he could delegate chores as his right as our father. Time honored patriarchal bullshit. I love my father. I followed orders due to the fact that I was a rent-free tenant rather than an obedient son. He wasn't present enough in my life to deserve that right, and I'm not so cold-hearted that I felt the need to remind him every time he exercised this mentality.

One day, he returned from work; "Son, take out this trash. Amethyst, wash these dishes." I took out the trash, and my sister hadn't even thought to budge. In all fairness, she was watching Nicholas Spark's *Notebook* on some television network. Anyway, my father noticed this and started yelling about the dishes so I began to do them. Suddenly, he went in the back room where Amethyst was, "Amethyst, I told you to do them dishes."

I followed him in, "Don't worry about it. Got it covered," but he was relentless in trying to get her to move.

Almost out of nowhere, Wendy begins yelling from the living room. Our house consisted of five separate rooms including the kitchen and the bathroom, so we heard her clearly, "You don't have to get her to do nothing for me. She can call her mama and go back home."

Then I interjected, screeching, "I can do the dishes!"

Wendy countered with, "Oh no, you've done too much already."

Belatedly, Amethyst rose from her corner on the carpet to wash the dishes in response to my father screaming and yelling about how ungrateful she was. Finally, they made their way to the sink and Amethyst vented, "I didn't make any of these *damn* dishes!"

This threw my father into a blind rage and he started pushing Amethyst in a corner screaming in anger as she cried and yelled in retort.

"You're staying in this house, who are you to disrespect me!" He roared.

"Get off me! You don't deserve respect. What have you done for us?" He had her by both arms backed into the wall.

And one thing above all things I feel my parents should know, even though they've tried their best, neither one of them were ever responsible enough to earn the right to put their hands on us. It felt unnatural and presumptuous of my father to delegate chores.

Somehow I inserted myself in between them, also yelling to be heard, told my father, "This is not okay, this is not okay," in an attempt to get him off her. He was saying he wasn't going to hurt her, but I didn't care. He hasn't earned the right.

In the midst of the whole debacle, Wendy called over my aunt who lived across the street, to try to defuse the situation. Sniffing out a juicy piece of drama was occurring, Aunt Darice rushed over with my two cousins Delsa and Jane, and she started trying to mediate the altercation after it passed. We all heard her without really listening, and that was that. I tried speaking with Amethyst and my father directly. Amethyst kept cutting me off, trying to tell my father how incompetent he was at being a father. Her exact words were, "you don't do anything for me." I would amend that to he hasn't done enough.

He responded, "I've done so much, don't say I've never done anything for you. I gave your mother so much money when we divorced—" That's the problem. They'd been divorced eleven years, and he was still living in the past. That night, he asked we all sit down and play a game of Spades. I complied. Amethyst and Wendy resisted at first, and I eventually got my sister to cave. Seeing the sadness in my father's eyes when he said, "I just thought we could use a little family time," hurt my heart. I appreciated his effort. We played Spades that evening in lieu of a peace treaty, and things were decent for a little while.

I'd clean daily, and when I was told that wasn't good enough, I cleaned more. I remained subordinate, and cleaned as was asked of me.

After I completed the tasks, I'd always ask Wendy if there was anything more she needed me to do, to clean, or anything she needed in general. I even mowed the lawn once. It was once, and I needed assistance starting the mower, but I stepped outside my comfort zone for that woman, including going outdoors.

One night about a week later, my father called a "family meeting" ('cause we're like the fucking Cosbys)[3]. I wasn't expecting the outcome. He began with Amethyst and I need to wake up earlier to suit Wendy's fancy, and I agreed and acknowledged this. I have always been nocturnal.

And Wendy huffed in her exhaustion, "I'm sorry, but when you told your dad you were coming, he should've told you no."

Quicker than the Dugger family could pop out another baby, heresy, sex scandal, or sanctimonious discrimination, the Amethyst-Wendy bitch-off resumed for round two after such a brief hiatus. Amethyst got up to leave, citing her early morning class the next day as the reason. My father convinced her to come back and hear Wendy out. Wendy continued her plea, "I need you to go. This isn't working out."

Instinctively, "Okay. I'm sorry you feel that way," I began dialing Diamond's number, hoping she'd come to pick me up to take me back to Farmville within the next week.

And, consistently Amethyst, Amethyst overreacted, "I don't need to listen to this." She started verbally fighting father.

Wendy's voice deeper, "Hold up, if you don't leave, I'm calling the police!" My father froze in shock.

Amethyst was about to get up and walk out when I told her, "Hold on! We can get a hotel room for the night if it comes to that." I was going to use part of my refund check from community college. I wasn't going to let my sister leave by herself in the middle of the night. Wendy repeatedly got in Amethyst's face and neither was backing down; I was busy wondering how many Hail Marys Amethyst would have to say if she bitch-slapped a cancer patient. By some miracle, it didn't come to that, and everything calmed down.

I didn't know what to do. The next day, I called my mother and asked if it was cool for me to return home, and her response was "Of course. You know wherever I am, you always have a home," but not before she

---

3 Which is probably truer than I care to admit.

gave me a speech about how weak my father is. "He practically has no spine," according to her. "He's like a jellyfish," and I couldn't help feeling like my moving and complying with all the nonsense Wendy said was equated to me turning into my father.

Throughout this madness, one of my best friends from high school, Karen Anghel, was there for me. She attended Christopher Newport University five miles from my father's house. We remained in contact and I visited her three times a week. Gracefully, she'd listen to all my problems despite my feeling bad for telling them to her. She's my Filipino Catholic therapist. Karen affirmed my fear that mostly I tend to do what's better for everyone, and that in this instance, I should put myself first. I'm afraid I'll turn into my mother, but I'm petrified of turning into my father, seeing that much of the damnation in his life has been earned. That's when I decided to keep my black ass right where it was.

The only time I really asserted myself to Wendy, face-to-face, happened after Amethyst had secured a room on campus after telling the staff her father's girlfriend kicked her out, which was partially true, but maybe not as dramatic as presented. Gloria, my father's best friend's girlfriend, asked me about something Wendy said, and I told her, "I don't know. I don't talk to Wendy." I did announce that with a bitchy undertone, but it was the truth. We had stopped speaking. Wendy wouldn't look at me, in my direction or anything, like I was some malicious creation making her life all the more unbearable. I gave up trying to be pleasant. Wendy knocked on the back room door ten minutes later, probably out of habit, before busting in the room furiously:

"Why did you tell my friend you don't talk to me?" Her voice thick as molasses.

"Because we don't talk."

"Oh... You didn't have to say it like that."

"Do you have a problem with me, Wendy?" I asked calmly.

"Hold up! Do you have a problem with *me*? This is *my* house!"

"I am not trying to argue with you, Wendy. I only asked a question because you seem angry."

"Well, yes, I have a problem with you. I told you last week I wanted you out of the house. Why are you still here?"

"My father said that is not an option. If you have a problem, you should probably take it up with him."

This is when I heard her sister, who knew me relatively well, in the background cosigning everything Wendy said. "Not an option?" her sister screeched in protest.

"Oh yeah. We gone fix this problem," Wendy asserted. She left, and I had to leave the house or things would've certainly escalated. I left out the back door to avoid seeing her, furthering her aggravation. Later that day I caught a bus to the mall like always. I received a call from my father like clockwork, and told him my side of what happened. At that point, he couldn't outright defend Wendy anymore. Earlier when she was trying to get me to leave, he had defiantly resolved, "She can leave!" I'll never know how that worked out, but later that day, he had a talk with her and she was to apologize to me, according to him. I never received an apology. One wasn't necessary. Her treating me better became enough, which again lasted about a week.

Soon she reverted to her old ways again. I was doing the dishes and I could hear her voice coming from my father's bedroom, arguing with him, making use of every vulgar profanity ever expressed. I had never even heard Wendy actually curse before. She'd say "dang" and "gosh dern." That was the closest she'd come to Showtime lingo before that night.

"Fuck fuck fuck! I don't give a fuck! You are fucking wrong!" And anything she could come up with, utilizing the "bitch" word. After verbally accosting my father, Wendy came out of the bedroom and into the kitchen where I tried to pretend I hadn't heard.

I said a shaky, "Hello," over my shoulder and her response was, "Don't say hello right fucking now." I was confused.

"But, what did I do?" My hands like vibrating prunes in the murky dishwater.

"You been talkin' 'bout my son!" She scowled.

I almost began crying because I didn't comprehend what was going on and would never talk about someone I had never even met. Met for five seconds maybe, but not someone I'd *never* met. I only judge the people I know (and entrepreneur, media mogul Kim Kardashian). She continued to yell incoherently. In between these utterances, she'd sing, "Put no shackles on my feet so I can dance," and then she'd return to cursing out my father. Wendy blamed my coughing and allergies for her cancer, and my something else trivial on her inability to win the lottery. It was close to midnight, and she kept insisting she needed to go to the hospital, and I thought she was having a psychogenic nonepileptic seizure because it was reminiscent of something similar I'd seen on *Grey's Anatomy*. Wendy kept saying she was going to call the police, and my father kept advising her not to. After half an hour, I thought it'd be a good idea to call and instruct them to bring an ambulance, something clearly wasn't right. Wendy, my father, and I confined ourselves to the living room, my father and I making covert eye contact, deciding to wait it out. Approximately an hour later, one of her sisters showed up and took Wendy to the hospital for the rest of the night.

The next day we assumed the cancer spread to her brain, or that's what Aunt Darice was banking on. Wendy was extremely erratic, and I had no idea what to do. Karen once advised me to "cuss her out." Since I'm a better Catholic than she is, I opted not to do so.

One morning, Wendy woke me up to iron my father's work shirt, which was dumb. He was nearly fifty and could iron his own shirt. I completed the task anyway and headed toward my grandmother's house across the street where she, my aunt, and cousins lived. I kept up this act of leaving for my grandmother's for two days before Wendy got pissed I wasn't helping her 24/7. Friends and family of hers would come over and notice Wendy's actions and her attitude toward me, we'd share a knowing look, maybe a shake of our heads, and continue our days. We knew at any rate Wendy didn't have long. We tried our best living around it. Once, Wendy mentioned she and my father were engaged. Initially, I thought her announcement was predicated on illusion, and yet my father confirmed their intent to marry and acknowledged his neglect to tell any of his children.

Wendy would become so enthralled it scared the shit out of me. She'd speak in a different octave and claim she was "coming to get" me and Amethyst. That her mother used to be a state trooper when she was alive, and her mom was still coming to get us. Wendy'd be less vehement around my father, but she wasn't the same in any vein. He knew she was going off the deep end; her eyes were as vacant and lifeless as she was soon to be. My father felt helpless.

Wendy approached me when I went to Walmart with my father, telling me I was going to die and I "ran for my life; I ain't grab no shoes or nothin' Jesus," if I may paraphrase Sweet Brown. I put on my shoes and told Karen I was coming to visit. Wendy frightened the fuck out of me when she started talking about her deceased parents coming to "get" me. One morning, after she demanded I mop and clean the bathroom, her sister came over to use the computer, the one who knew me relatively well and acted as Wendy's backup cosigner. I told her what was happening. Before everything was in full swing, I loaned Wendy twenty dollars and was concerned about retrieving it. I spoke with her sister about that, and more importantly, Wendy communicating with the dead.

Having suspicions of our conversation, Wendy began listening in, abruptly bringing the exchange to a halt. Thankfully my grandmother called, requesting my assistance. A little later that day, Wendy's sister came by my grandmother's house and told us Wendy is bipolar and has been for years. Every few years, she'd go off her meds and asks for money from everyone to go to bingo. She even petitioned tight-fisted Aunt Darice for money, so I knew she was actually exponentially desperate. There goes my twenty, I thought. Her sister went on to say that my coming up to stay with her was added pressure she didn't need, and this could've all been avoided if Wendy had informed my father of her preexisting illness and the possible consequences that accompany it. Her sister went on to state that she'd spoke about it with her family, and for my safety, it'd be best if I not stay there with Wendy until they could get her medicine under control. I obliged, as my grandmother allotted me her couch for the time being. I only ever went back across the street to collect clothes when I knew it was safe.

A month later, my father told me I had an open invitation to return, and that Wendy had been requesting me. I ended up returning, and as I moved back in, she returned my twenty dollars. Wendy became even more dependent, and I helped her. I even sat and watched television with her a time or two, and Karen's roommates were pleased to hear I didn't need nearly as many emergency visits. Wendy would constantly ask me to open sodas for her, then she'd go to the bathroom minutes later. I figured she needed water, but I'm not going to deny a cancer patient a grape Fanta if she desires one.

Once, I suggested she drink water and she thanked me for my concern, but continued with soda. A week of that lifestyle left her resembling death. I was in my father's room with him, searching for socks. When we emerged, Wendy was sprawled out on the couch, her eyes blackened, cheeks sunken, and mouth agape. He thought she was dead. Only after a beat did we see her chest rise, and I urged my father to call her son, who hadn't stopped by nearly enough.

That was the same day I found out I was accepted into Christopher Newport University, and I had a mini celebration with my younger cousin, Jane, at my grandmother's house. That evening, my grandmother returned from walking about the neighborhood in the nosey manner in which she does daily, and told us there was an ambulance at my father's house. Wendy's family members surrounded the block with their cars—she has fifteen sisters and the most I'd ever seen at once were four or five; she'd had cancer since 2007. The paramedics strapped Wendy to a gurney and loaded her in the truck. While there was still time, I stole my father's phone, found her son's number, and dialed. As peacefully as I could, I told him his mother was being taken to the emergency room. Choking back tears, thinking as I told him, "If it were my mother, I'd want to know." Wendy's brother took the phone from me, I was unaware of the details, and informed her son that he'd come to pick him up and take him to his mother as soon as possible.

I also called Amethyst and told her I didn't suspect Wendy had long, maybe two weeks. No one said this, but judging from the state she was in that morning, it was all I could conclude. Walking back into the house after everyone accompanying her to the hospital left, I discovered Wendy was a bipolar cancer patient yet to be diagnosed with diabetes. The signs were there, but cancer supersedes diabetes and I thought dehydration was another side effect of advanced chemo and radiation.

Instead of walking back to my grandmother's as I wished, my father requested I stay at his home and hold down the fort until he could return. That's when I began internalizing exactly what my father was feeling. One day the week before, my father peculiarly stopped by my grandmother's house and asked if everything was okay with Wendy. Being my normal self-absorbed self, I paid no attention to the tears in his eyes or that crack in his voice until Aunt Darice and cousin Delsa pointed it out to me. I went out to the porch and asked him what was wrong.

As tears fell, "She's going to die." She hadn't been looking well for a long time, and I guess I never fully considered what this meant for him. He's fifty; his best friend died a few years before, and now his fiancée. I had no idea how to comfort him. The only deaths I have reference with happened to those who had lived full lives, and I could not fathom losing one of my friends or a loved one, and I don't want to. I don't know how my father was able to deal with it every day. Maybe he isn't all that weak after all. His tears fell and he began a continuous exhale of grief. That night when Wendy was diagnosed as diabetic, he returned home and everyone left assured that Wendy was going to make it through the night. My father closed the front door and lit up a blunt.

Two days after she went into the hospital, Wendy was released. She requested I stay at my grandmother's house one night, then I returned to assist with her well-being the next. Her son soon started showing up regularly, and personally thanked me for telling him what was going on. I'm guessing his mother downplayed everything as she always did whenever she was in pain or needed/wanted anything. One particular evening, Wendy came into the back room and told me, "I'm going to have to give you some money or something for you helping me."

"Oh Wendy, you don't have to do that," I replied, lying in bed.

"I do. You've been helping me so much, I gotta give you something, at least one hundred dollars when my check comes in." I knew that second what it was to care for a terminally ill person. They don't say thank you. They aren't very gracious, and the only gratitude they show is rare because they don't know how to die and they don't know how to get used to it. They don't know how to be helped when nothing is going to help them forget death. Wendy Fish, after four months, told me she appreciated my work for her, and that's what authentic validation feels like. She wasn't able to give me one hundred dollars, or any money to be exact, but her thinking of me was worth more than any money I could have ever received from her. Must've been something about me; my mother's a nurse, and she helps people transition all the time. While most of my former classmates were enjoying their first college parties, I was opening soda cans for someone who lacked fingernails, and it was a privilege to be her can opener for time I was allotted the chance, and what a lucky break.

My maternal grandmother's demise is the only death to have a lasting effect on my life. She went away when I was six years old; I assumed she had to leave because my mother was getting remarried and that Wilbert wouldn't have wanted her in his house. What I as a child couldn't understand, or what wasn't explained very well to me, is that my grandmother had hit a certain age needing round-the-clock care, and my mother had a full-time job she had to keep as a newly divorced woman, and my siblings had to go to school during the day. I was so young I don't remember much. I remember her heart was kind and I know how she'd make me feel.

Albeit irregularly in those days, I'd wake up to discover everyone in my house gone, except for my grandma in her room all the way in the back of the house. I'd get in bed with her and she'd tell me stories she heard when she was a little girl. We'd talk and laugh until my parents returned home. No, I can't remember everything, and it sucks, but I remember feeling safer and loved than I ever felt in my entire life, and that's gone now, and I'll probably never feel that way again.

I don't know what she'd think of me now—if she'd be proud of the man I've become, or if she'd renounce me because of my sexuality, but at six, I knew the kind of love I've never had to question. That's something my parents have never afforded me. Other family members, friends, even Amethyst, I would argue, all wanted something from me. My grandmother loved me for me, and I'm there's nothing better I'll experience in this lifetime than being loved by her. No, I don't remember most things, but I remember what her love was like: like receiving a gift for being alive, every day. And I'm not sure; I'm hoping I still have some of it in me.

Relate back to Wendy, who has less than six months to live, and I think she was that to somebody. Someone felt that loved by her and she'll never even know her grandkids. She won't ever see her gay son with the man of his dreams. She has to leave this world so early she can't even watch her son graduate college. That is real pain. I speak with my father more often now, forgiving him of his shortcomings and looking past all the disappointment over the years, because he's going to need someone in his corner as he stares death in the face, in the eyes of the woman he loves. He told me Wendy requested me to come see her before she passes, maybe to thank me, or possibly because she appreciates my presence, and I will try to do that for her because that is what she deserves. I think about my grandmother and how she lived. I try living in a way she'd be infinitely proud of, so if Wendy wants me to hold her hand, I will hold her hand. One silver lining in all this: perhaps their energy, their souls, Wendy's and my grandmother's, will cross one another along their intended wavelengths. My father's girlfriend is dying; she deserves the world and more.

Eight: Almonds

It's been a while since I've written anything. When all you have to write about lately regards parenting, alcoholism, and cancer-related death, it tends to take a toll on your soul. Writing is cathartic, yes, but I'll be damned if it doesn't drag your heart up and down the interstate to be run over by tractor trailers in the process. And it is a *fucking* process. I practically need assurance and a steel vagina (I'd say a brass set of balls, but in reality, vaginas have proven much more likely to withstand pain and maintain endurance. For instance, sometime in your life you'll either hear about, or personally experience, erectile dysfunction. According to WebMD, it is common amongst 5 percent of forty-year-old men and between 15 and 25 percent of men aged sixty-five or older. However, I have yet, in my nineteen years, encountered a woman of any age complaining about her vagina's inability to open. Which I assume means they're more reliable as well. Vaginas: They open every time!) in order to write this damn thing!4 Enough bitching outta me. Here goes... I think...

In examining areas of my life that would aid my understanding identity, and wherever the fuck to go from here, I have to examine the people who have witnessed my emergence as the flamboyant fixture that may be seen today, or the people who have guided me when I became lost, or the people who have simply remained in my life, which is certainly a feat in its own right. I haven't been a lotus flower blossoming under the vibrant permanent pacifying rays of the ever-burning sun. I've been *that* daisy, the polluted one poking up from concrete, half eaten by a deranged city rat.

These are the people who have helped me get through shit:

---

4 The closed vagina was a minor plot point on an episode of *Masters of Sex*. I still doubt it's as common as whiskey dick.

My ninth grade English teacher, Debbie Fast, suggested (demanded) I try out for the drama team. I had always been interested in acting, never really finding the opportunity aside from one line in a partially memorable fifth grade Christmas musical. Newly married Mrs. Hill could've made me a star; instead she chose a ginormous freckled skinny thespian over me, and ever since, I lost all hope in my dreams to become the next Fran Drescher. It all turned on its head one early September afternoon right after school...

"Waldell, get up there and read for Paw," Fast demanded nonchalantly, as she had already mentally cast me in that role. I must note it was impeccable. Before that, all the acting ability I had ever shown was reading aloud in her class. I like to think I made the *Epic of Gilgamesh* all the more enchanting.

"Uh, um, actually I had planned to do stuff behind the scenes. I don't think I'm a very good actor." That's close enough to the timid bullshit I spewed. The year before that, I was bombarded with being called "Gaylord,"[5] and I subsequently wanted to seriously coast in sustained unrecognizability.

"No. Get up there and read." Fast's vision was impenetrable, and I was too inferior to argue with that woman on a mission. Frankly stated, she could not be stopped. I did as I was told, walking up the old, decaying steps to the stage, holding the photocopied script in my hand. I was shaking so fiercely I wondered if I still possessed speaking ability, and even if I did, how in the hell was I to produce sound. Fast, hearing vocalized chirps erupting from my diaphragm, I was cast as Paw in my very second school play, and I had more than one line.

It was exhilarating to get to be part of something, having been decidedly outcast in five school systems prior to my Drama Team family. I felt important and accepted, and I gained a few pals along the way. Safe, clean fun, I could've been Nancy Reagan's poster child for any campaigning propaganda she needed to sell. This was where I met Khiry Palmer—the foremost high-priestess drama bitch of them all, Katisha Sargent—the radiant African-American princess, Erin Ganset and Nicole Hayes—the unsung sheroes of drama geeks everywhere, who barely ever had any lines but never missed rehearsal, Carter Chassey—future president of these United States and maybe Guam, Karen Anghel,

---

5 My apologies, we never agreed on spelling.

and Carol Forkes. I knew Carol from class, where I sat with the rebellious Rebecca Bowman aka Max, and I had only *heard* of Karen, the busty Filipina girl who smiles a lot, as every other red-blooded teen male in Prince Edward County High School knew and discussed at length. I didn't get what the hoopla was about. She was pretty, but I wasn't killing myself to get with that or anything. She just seemed like a decent person to talk to backstage while preparing for my entry, "Preacher Hagla comin' up the trail!" with all the bravado I could muster. In my head, I performed with Morgan Freeman's elegance and Samuel L. Jackson's distinction. I spoke to Karen with ease, without any want to get in her pants, even though many years later, I managed to do just that; happy to report her jeans look better on me.

Carol Johanson Forkes was an immediate force to be reckoned with. The bitch put the steel in steel vagina, and had a surplus of brains to accompany such a commanding piece of machinery. She, in other words, was a badass mother fucker, and though you enjoyed whenever she'd seldom speak out in class (which occurred more frequently as time went on and we realized we were never growing out of our awkward phase, determined only to embrace it more), you hoped whichever quip she'd come up with, seemingly with minimal effort involved, wouldn't be at your expense. She's the girl who corrected the teacher without batting an eyelash while probably playing Tetris on her phone underneath the desk. Carol was the girl every man knew he couldn't have and lacked the intelligence to compete with. A few times she called me out on an unfunny joke (I'm very often a tirelessly corny person) and I took it like a man because I knew I'd be ruined if Carol slayed me in front of the world, and I'd be forced to live with shame and perpetual humiliation for the four years of high school I had till graduation. It didn't matter that she had no upper body strength or that she'd get winded running from one end of the room to the other. She was Carol Forkes, and you didn't fuck with her. So when she asked me to be her friend, I squealed and said, "Of course!"

We were in tenth grade, and Ms. Fast (never married) asked for volunteers to assist running the concession stand for the Homecoming football game. Carol and Karen signed up, and I said I would, but didn't have a ride. Carol suggested that I volunteer with her and Karen later that evening, while after school, we'd go to Carol's to hang before heading out. That was the first time it hit that Carol liked talking to me, that I was intriguing enough for her prestigious highness. I felt a tingling sensation. Everywhere. Who the hell am I kidding? I was balls-out giddy.

Her mother's friend, Emily, picked us up, and the traveling conversation went swimmingly:

"He has a great butt!" I declared.

"Can we not look at guys' butts?" Carol protested. (Hindsight is always twenty-twenty.)

"Hey, if it's nice, it's nice," countered Karen.

"Seriously, Carol, where else am I supposed to look?" I whined.

"Oh God, you guys are so embarrassing in front of my mom's friend!" Carol wailed.

"Oh, it's fine!" Emily said through her giggles. "I'm used to it." She works at Longwood University; it's very gay.

Once we arrived at Carol's, I was awed by her house. Surely, it was the most well-decorated home I had ever seen in real life, with the most comfortable brown leather sofas my ass has ever been acquainted with. The steadiest article of furniture pulling everything together was a humongous lamp shaped like a light bulb in the corner by the television. There were books everywhere: books on the shelves, books on the floor, books in the kitchen, books on the table, books sprawled strategically along the staircase—I wouldn't have been surprised if they stashed a few in the refrigerator to save some room. It was so innovative and current, I felt as if I was stepping into a moving art design once past the threshold. Karen went directly for the fridge, and Carol dove for the remote.

We watched *Supernatural* and Karen and I took turns popping Carol's mom, Johanson's, gourmet almonds into our mouths, thinking they must taste better than a leftover copy of *Moby Dick,* peacefully passing time until we were ready to leave to work the concession stand. Two and a half episodes in, Karen ran upstairs to wash her hair or nap or something or other, and Carol and I were left alone. Here lay the moment of truth; could I somehow make it work, here, in her home that could've just as easily been 2009s Studio 54? Could I cement my friendship with the unrefuted Queen of Comebacks? It was easier than I would've dreamt.

She looked at me, and with eagerness in her voice and the slightest hesitancy in her tone, said, "I think I would kiss a girl."

I wasn't expecting that, this being my first time in Wonderland, she would confide something of that nature to me. "Oh? Why is that?" General confusion in my voice evoking quite the facial expressions, I imagine.

"I don't know. I just feel like it's something I should do." She didn't say it like a lesbian. What I mean by that is, she didn't tell me she wanted to kiss a girl like it was this newly found revelation, like she was coming out the closet. She admitted this like a girl who was curious about kissing other women, and that by no means makes anyone gay. More people should experiment in order to save themselves grave heartache down the road. And my fifteen-year-old self was nothing close to astonished about the confidence she placed in me.

"Okay," I said. I was in. I was becoming one of them, and it was a sealed deal because Carol admitted something she purposely chose to share with me when Karen was out of the room, in a way that I understood was private enough to keep only between us. Cann[6] has said that she doesn't remember that, but it was a big moment for me. It was one of the first times I didn't feel like a reject, more like a recurring guest with character growth potential. Carol became more human to me, and for thirty seconds, I stopped trying to win her approval and listened to her, something she needed more than anything, a nonjudgmental listener who might understand where she was coming from.

Half an episode later, Karen pranced down the stairs, hair shining luminously and it was time for the Homecoming game. Nirvana and her husband arrived to take us back to Prince Edward to volunteer. The next time I went to Carol's house, I was met with Johanson's bitter animosity. "Who ate all my damn almonds?" Karen couldn't help but point fingers.

---

[6] More on Cann, later.

Nine: My Sim Family

As a young child, not having many friends and mostly left to my own devices, I built up quite an unhealthy addictive mentality toward the virtual living game, *The Sims*. While most seven-year-olds played outside, or maybe played video games more age appropriate like *Legend of Zelda, Crash Bandicoot*, or *Grand Theft Auto: The Graphic, Misogynistic, Excessively Violent Game That Has Limited Roles For Women Which Has Probably Indoctrinated the Youth of America to Becoming Mass Murders Without Consciences*, or the one my father enjoyed playing with me the most, *True Crimes*—the one with the white cop who'd forcefully frisk black prostitutes.

The desire to play such a game as *The Sims* came into effect at age seven. It was after my parents' separation, and therapists would probably tell me I was obsessed with creating the perfect family because mine suffered from an uneven balance after checks of love returned null-and-void on all accounts. I love to tell stories. Playing around the house with Amethyst, portraying her son (which happened to be a stand-in Raggedy Ann doll when I was otherwise preoccupied), and her mother whenever the scene called for it. I liked the latter role much more. There was something about that characterization that drew me in indefinitely. Not to mention all the times we devised Barbie plots with gravely realistic repercussions. They got pregnant and had miscarriages whenever we played with them. God, we watched *a lot* of television back then. One time, Black Barbie died of cancer and I'm sure white Barbie must've been raped at least once.

From what my reasoning can make of it, there was never any pressure for me to create the perfect family because the perfect family didn't exist. The creation of sweeping dramas were my motive. Not the boring ones, the ones full of delicious secrets and over-the-top plots. I appreciated a good soap opera. Long live *The Guiding Light.*[7]

---

7 This was the title prior to 1975, when it changed to *Guiding Light*.

I became rather good at building a family and maintaining their bliss so they might more successfully pursue other aspects of their all-important Sim lives. The time I purchased the horrendously tacky bed that allowed the adults to engage in sexual activity, it was a wrap and I considered myself an aficionado. Here I was, wondering why I was an outcast for 90 percent of my life, and the closest I had come to sex at fifteen was internet porn and building a family on a game that shouldn't have been suitable for small children—a computer-animated family that spoke in awkward sounds except for the occasional "Booger snot"—was my standard Friday night. Back then I thought I was hot shit. Now I have *Scandal* and I can see how ridiculous I *used* to be.

Although I enjoyed the game and dallying in an alternate universe where I could be whomever I desired to be (mainly in the army because it paid two hundred fifty dollars a day—you just couldn't beat that), I cannot stop myself pondering on how easy it was to erase what you didn't wish to further exist. A few weeks ago, I jokingly tweeted that "I have the type of family you'd delete off *The Sims*." Nothing provoked my sending that. I love my family and wouldn't dare delete them for anything. Besides, I may need a kidney one day. On the other hand, sometimes it gets to be too much, and I can't really say in those moments that I don't wish things were different.

I don't like it when my mother disappears for twenty-four hours at a time. I say I don't worry about it or that she's a grown woman whom I am sure is safe, or my favorite line, "I DON'T KNOW HER LIFE!" It's really starting to worry me. Maybe that's coming with age. When I was younger and she disappeared, I don't think I was nearly as concerned as I truly am now, not in comparison to Amethyst, who always presumes the worst.

You can't recede into yourself and hide in your own private thoughts when your oldest sister calls you every couple of hours asking if your mother has returned home. I know eventually Mother's going to return, and that it is probably none of my business where she's been since I am technically her *adult* son. The truth is no matter how old you get, you never stop worrying about the well-being of your parents, even when you'd like to.

It's not my place to ask her where she's been or to make a big fuss that I'm glad she's safe. In reality, I'm angrier than I allow to be seen. I act like nothing's happened and smile my way through welcoming her home, secretly wondering where the hell she's been or why she couldn't call. It feels rude when family comes to visit and we literally stay up the entire night waiting for her, and she doesn't even send a text.

Randomly, she'll pull into the drive and there's no grand explanation for her delay, not that it's necessarily owed to me. People who've actually traveled to see her, waiting for her to arrive, deserve the most consideration. I simply feel unappreciated. If it weren't for a few friends in the Farmville area, I don't think I'd return home as often as I do. I do not feel wanted there by my mother.

These are the thoughts that race through my mind at night when she comes home, finally. To myself, with my eyes closed and beckoning sleep, I couldn't help wishing for a Sim family and I could start anew if I wanted, with a family that loved each other, instead of tolerating one another's company when we'd prefer a check in the mail and a phone call once a month assuring ourselves each other is alive.

I know we love one another and carry each other in our hearts. I don't feel that always, and it's becoming harder to mask what I need to, and how I really feel, as I have all these years. My mother was about to drive drunk one night to pick her friend up from the airport in Richmond, an hour and a half from our house, and my sisters were all a tizzy. Amethyst took the keys from her and Mother kept berating her, threatening to cut off service to her cell phone, which she has done before. My stepfather continued his charade, doing his best to turn a blind eye, and I spoke up and told Amethyst to give the keys to her because Mother was just going to get meaner.

Minutes later, Diamond called and screamed into the phone, perturbed as to why I was reacting to the situation as if it was normal and happened regularly. Mother's attempt to drive drunk didn't, her drunken rampages did. My stepfather recalled at a later date that she unplugged the refrigerator, determined to leave him. Like she was going to single-handedly lift the refrigerator and stuff it into her Nissan.

The whole debacle subsided after Amethyst relinquished the keys and threatened to call the cops if Mother went anywhere. Amethyst marched into the computer room where I was perched, illegally streaming some show, and shouted:

"I don't know how you got like this. It's like your soul is so hardened. Nothing makes you feel anything." At times, I have said the greatest character I have created has been my mother; the greatest role I've ever played has been *me* in every day of my life, and it feels a little dangerous since I'm thinking of retiring *my* act.

That seemed like the dumbest and most vile thing a person could ever do to themselves, lie naked in their candor. That's when someone is their most vulnerable, and someone could really offend. I have to protect myself and keep my heart guarded.

And still, why maintain such an ostentatious precedence when I'm quickly growing tired of trying to be someone I'm not?

I need to run, not away from everything, but away from my mother. I don't think either one of us is ready for an honest relationship, and if I'm going to be honest with someone, I don't want it to be with someone who has the capacity to counter-punch with such ferocity. I highly doubt she *intentionally* would; it is still too scary to take the chance. I'll wait till I'm older and financially independent, and discover what it feels like to reveal myself completely to someone before drawing back that curtain on my dear mother.

Self-protection is always a primary motivator, concurrent with my homeostasis hypothesis. I believe that no matter what happens to me, emotionally I can entertain a state of preservation within. It's BS, but it helps me sleep at night.

My family isn't perfect like the kind I could create on a video game. They're all I have to be proud of, and I am. I don't know how I'm going to cope with my own shortcomings any longer. I'm hoping they'll be there picking the thorns from my wounds when I inevitably fall and disgrace myself. Worse comes to worst, it's not like they can delete me.

Ten: Nature Made You a Dick

Karen Linda Eve Agcaoili Anghel has always been endowed with a rather large mouth. It's partly what made her and me rather great and easy friends from the start of our relationship. She was loud; I was louder. I spoke more; she spoke faster. When it came to other people's business, and this I believe is why we became as close as we have, we enjoyed listening, but we LIVED for telling it largely to one another. Except for deep personal indiscretions, like a closeted best friend[8] etc. For the longest time, I hadn't the slightest idea that Karen could have ever in her life happened to talk about me.

It was an ordinary day for us. It was after school, and we were rehearsing for the drama team. We stayed from 3:30 p.m. till 5 p.m., and not a special practice lasting from 3:30 p.m. till 6 p.m. Her mother walked through the doors of the auditorium with a commanding subtlety that warranted a second glance. If you didn't look at her twice, you were blind, and I'm a gay man.

The setting sun kissed her ever flowing jet-black hair, which graced her shoulders and back without it ever overcompensating or distracting from her natural features. Feminine but firm in a way that's been blessed with great years and fortunate genetics, her prominent cheekbones fixed perfectly, bringing her face to a flawless smile. Her eyes wise with years but doused with good-natured charm, open to the charities life afforded when tapping into a rare elegance grasped only by few individuals for passing moments of incomparable beauty.

"That's my mom," Karen said, like I was going to figure she was anyone else's. Our school is virtually zero percent Asian, and this lady certainly wasn't Martha Stewart or Vivica A. Fox.

Slowly, I made my way over to the statuesque vision, silently hoping she'd deem me worthy of her presence. Smiling, I introduced myself, "Hello, I'm Waldell Goode!"

---

[8] The only secret I've ever actually kept in my life. Guess who!

She looked at me, beaming, brushing off my personally brave introduction. As if I looked up and noted the sky as being blue, she replied in a similar tone, "Oh, I know who you are!" And she hugged me. That was weird.

Of all my knowledge regarding Karen and her ability to recount any story, person, or situation as a highly detailed anecdote, I had never thought in a billion years anything I had done would've been worth recounting. That wasn't the most interesting thing either; her mother embraced *me*. Maybe I had seen her once at a function very briefly and she knew who I was. Granted, I'm sure Karen told them all about the "bisexual" kid on the team, who's actually freakishly gay, like probably the gayest guy on Earth, like gayer than a Republican scandal gay, and therein lies what I didn't understand.

Karen *talked* to her parents! I had no idea people did that. Of course I've heard of people having good relationships with their families, but to be totally honest with them? To tell them about your day like they were invested in your life? To have a relationship where you have a friend they haven't formally met before, and they easily could identify him based on the lengthy descriptions about said person? That was new to me, and though seemingly unnatural, it worked for this oddly large family who genuinely *liked* one another. The only sense I was able to make from that whole encounter is they aren't American. That just isn't what Americans do.

Several months later and I was able to gain a decent amount of perspective. I met Karen's father. If my mother is one of my greatest characters, her father has to be the only one giving her competition. He's the guy you read about in books, the kind who goes into fights and walks out with drinking buddies, lifelong friends who'll offer him a kidney if his were ever ruined by drinking—then after the surgery, they'd go out and buy drinks for other people because they couldn't drink anymore.

Pete Anghel accepts people as they are and encourages individuality. As I've noted, he's not American. For instance, I went to the movies with Karen, crashing one of Katherine's, her little sister's, middle school dates (who's a college freshman now, which makes no sense) when Karen's father boldly announced in front of everyone, "Waldell, I could outgay you." This was when I was in my hardcore David Bowie phase. I was wearing makeup, skinny jeans, and a lady's ruffled blouse, and here was this forty-year-old Asian man, with a gorgeous wife and four kids, threatening to "outgay" me. I called his bluff and naturally ate my own words when Pat Anghel outgayed Waldell Goode on Katherine's middle school date at the movies, and it was a night I never forgot. I never knew a grown man's hips could pop so much. He sashayed like the Sunchase parking lot was a runway. He could flick his wrists faster than I could bat an eyelash. And to be honest, I took notes.

Over the years, I have come to look deeply into their home life and the contentment they have with one another. Many years later when Karen and I were discussing where we'd want to attend university, she said she wanted to go in-state so she wouldn't be too far from her family. I looked at her like she was stupid. It wasn't my intention. When I thought about going to college, I aspired to get as far away from my family as I could. Karen and I were looking from completely different states of origin. If I were Karen, planning to go in-state would've made more sense considering how close they'd always been. I didn't have similar feelings with my family. I wanted to be free from all things and begin an entirely new existence.

I hadn't known how close I became to the Anghels until I was discussing having someone give me away should I ever marry. A long time ago, I asked my father and he said he wasn't interested. I ended up telling Amethyst that maybe I'd get Mr. Anghel to do it.

She looked at me and lamented, "I don't think you should put them on a pedestal. They're not perfect. Trust and believe they have problems just like everyone else."

To which I replied, "Oh I'm sure. I really don't think they're perfect, nobody's perfect. I just like them for the people they are."

"And Maine, that's fine, but you shouldn't put them on a pedestal when you're always bringing down mama. That's not fair to her. I know we didn't have perfect childhoods, but we always had heat and food and TV... most of the time." I'm guessing she's had a while to think about this.

I will not lie and say there was no truth to what Amethyst was saying; I do regularly take little digs at Mother and that isn't right. I don't even realize I'm doing it when I say things like, "Maybe she can give me away if she won't be drunk at the time," as if I was expecting my own mother to be drunk at my wedding. This encouraged my understanding that I was focusing on the negative so keenly in my mother, I was desperately seeking out kindness from other people. I can't bring myself to apologize for that. Humanity should seek kindness in all that exists. This conversation made me see I should find the goodness and love at home that I saw very easily spending a short sabbatical with the Anghels.

I rapidly learned that Amethyst was willing to pinpoint my flaws as a cover for her own insecurities. One Thursday, Amethyst and I sat down to watch *Scandal* and my father was getting high with his friends outside as he does all the time. In his "elevated" state, he came in and sat on the couch, informing Amethyst and me, "You guys don't know how to have fun."

We've always been atypical kids, Amethyst and me, and Amethyst's always been the most sensitive one of us. When our father comes in and gives an inebriated soliloquy, I've learned to ignore him, especially since Wendy's death is still so recent. Amethyst felt he was judging us (which he was) so she got up and left the room and he followed her. Big mistake.

"Can you get away from me when you're like this?" Amethyst pleaded.

"Like what, Amethyst? I am not high," my father countered. He'd definitely been smoking; I can't really determine whether or not that constituted him being high, seeing as I didn't know how to have fun and all, and I was hoping they'd shut the fuck up so I could finish watching *Scandal*.

"I don't like you when you're like this." I could tell in a few minutes it was about to get ugly.

"You don't like me anyway," he continued. That wasn't a fair comeback. This showed deeper personal issues above and beyond his current state of insobriety, but I'll let Dr. Phil write that book.

The tiff escalated astronomically fast, and Amethyst made her way around to, "My other friends' dads don't do this. They don't smoke or get high! Why can't you be like them?"

Those six words together are the most terrible thing a person you care about can ask you. He boyishly replied, "Because I'm not them!" And stomped out of the house, heated. I told her she needed to apologize. I give my father shit, and it's well-deserved shit, but no one deserves to be compared to someone else. While Amethyst is the most sensitive of all of us, she is still the most stubborn like our dad.

I knew I loved them. I cherished their ideals of family and maybe later would seek to model my family after their formula, because whatever it is, it works. Withal, not once have I ever wished any one of my parents were Jennifer or Pete. I have no remorse for my parents not being like them; I love my mother and my father as separate people, and if I want them to change, I want them to be better versions of themselves, not shadows of people they could never be because they're not them. My father could never be Pete Anghel, and likewise, Pete Anghel could never be my father (which I'm thankful for due to a latent crush I shall never speak of), nor would I wish that for either one of them. That is an unrealistic and unfair demand a person should never place on another person.

Beautiful things are possible when people are accepted as they are. Recently at a bonfire, Karen's dad shared his excitement that Cann and I are Karen's best friends. It doesn't bother him that Cann and I are not straight and root for our own respective teams, because he knows we're good people. When Cann realized she was lesbian, it took her a year before she felt comfortable telling the Anghels, even though they've made a large show of loving people as they are, to prevent making anyone feel like they need to hide their identity.

Cann was nervous, as is reasonable for anybody admitting to a new, some would say drastic, development in their personal lives. Plus the Anghels are Catholic, but that didn't stop Pete from showing me out in front of the movie theater. He took a break from telling the stories he always tells from his time in university, writing plays starring straight guys and gays side-by-side—which I've heard at least five times but always listened because he is the world's best storyteller—to tell me of one of his once trans-identifying friends.

He told me that his friend, X, was at a real crossroads, still deciding which gender was appropriate for him, and there was no clear answer at that time. X had been living in America as a woman. He returned to the Philippines as suggested by his mother to reconnect with his roots. When he arrived, he connected with his old self and became even more conflicted when talking with Pete. X seemed to be stuck on the fact that nature made him a man, and that is when Mr. Anghel corrected his lost friend, "Nature made you a dick; nature didn't make you a man." I wouldn't know how that affected X's decision, who decided to not have the surgery. It certainly meant a great deal to me. Pete knew that sex and gender are two different entities, and a penis does not define who a person is. He made sure X arrived at a decision with the knowledge sex is between the legs and gender lies between the ears. That was in the 90s.

We were more than bodies freezing in early June. We were souls that understood each other. That singular statement was so much deeper than any logic, and was inundated with such foolproof profundity, that I felt something reminiscent that left me a thousand years ago. I felt truly accepted and loved for who I was, for the nature of my inner workings and the little piece of God that dwells within all of us. I feel like he found the light the Little Match Girl inside of me had been carrying, looking for kindness, enabling the flame to burn brighter in a way I was so wishing it could. I felt connected and so purely loved that night I went home and wanted to cry; people don't connect like that anymore. I knew it was rare.

I am the little engine that could. Jennifer is the voice whispering in my ear, saying that she knows I can. I am a little drummer boy and Mr. Anghel is the one who shows me how to play correctly, and even louder, and I love them because they've loved me first and have made it truly easy for me. I am the kid who crossed the road, probably because the Anghels helped him get to the other side, and I owe them for the years and the meals and the rides and the advice that helped me look forward, and also make me think I'm not only going to be okay, I'm going to be fan-fucking-tastic, and *never* alone!

Eleven: My Blaine

I love you. In a really big, really big 'pretend to like your taste in music, let you eat the last piece of cheesecake, hold a radio over my head outside your bedroom window, unfortunate way that makes me hate you' love you. So pick me. Choose me. Love *me.*
– Shonda Rhimes

I'm in love with Derek Island. I don't even know why I'm admitting this. Right now I'm listening to "Moments" by One Direction and I'm just really in my feels. I've denied it a trillion times to Karen, and even more so to myself. I think it needs to be expressed. The depths of my gratitude for him being in my life reaches far beyond my expectations, much to the detriment of any rational thought I can formulate on the subject. Said feelings have become exceedingly bothersome given that one's best friend obnoxiously repeats to no end, "He looooooooovessssss you" and you want, in spite of yourself, to believe her. There is no substantial reasoning for these emotions, and they, like most teen angsty heartfelt trifles, will dissipate in time. And I'll look back half a century later, living in an empty house with a cat that I'm probably allergic to, and laugh at my once naïve dream to live a life of uninhibited bliss with the man I love and the future children we'd adopt together. Then a *Golden Girls* rerun will come on, I'll turn up my hearing aid and yell to geriatric Karen to pump up the volume. Life as a senior citizen is sure to be grand.

This newfound love has a genesis, beginning with Derek asking me if I'd seen *Not Another Gay Movie*, a parody of *Not Another Teen Movie*, which is a parody of blockbuster films centered around teenage protagonists. A parody film of a parody film, and one of the gayest works of art ever created, and yeah, I'd seen it. He then texted me that one of the characters reminded him of me, which I found pretty astounding since the entire film featured a foursome of Caucasian teens all looking to get laid; I'm black, and I make sure to exert little to no interest in finding another sexual partner. I've decided to focus my efforts on being single and content loving something that pleasured me all hours of the day and night, rarely ever disappointing—Netflix. Of the four characters, there was one who ended up losing his virginity in a threesome by way of double penetration. One had a thing for GILFS, (Grandpas I'd Like to Fuck) and the other two characters were friends who ended up discovering their love for one another and flip-flop screwing[9] by an outdoor built-in pool.

I assumed Derek meant on my journey through life I'd be sexually liberated and end up a freelance sex worker at a nursing home, or that I have one of the world's most stretchable holes. I was wrong. He said that I reminded him of one of the friends that ended up with the other one. Further I pressed, thinking that he meant he thought we were going to shag each other by a pool, which I wouldn't have been entirely opposed to. His reply intrigued me. Dare said that it wasn't because he thought we'd have flip-flop sex, one of the reasons being he sees me strictly as a bottom, and that he feels it's inevitable for us to end up together.

I told him that I was beginning to think he subconsciously desired such an ending. It wasn't the first time he'd shared this particular thought with me. His reply was, "I wouldn't mind ending up with you" and this fucked me up. Instantaneously, I began believing that someone wanted me because they "wouldn't mind" ending up with me—if they didn't have any other options. Maybe that says a lot about me. Maybe it indicates a life in front of Netflix isn't all I told myself it was cracked up to be. Maybe I'm as desperate for love as the rest of them, slightly better at hiding it, or avoiding the conversation in order to pretend my emotions aren't real and I'm just as strong without anyone as a person is with a perfect relationship, because *codependency is for losers*. Maybe I pretend being alone doesn't suck so I don't have to realize that my best option thus far is a friend who "wouldn't mind" having to end up with me. I decided I shouldn't dwell on the pain lodged behind the false presentation of how I truly feel. All the scars will be there to remember and live through tomorrow.

Hearing of Dare's suggestion, my mind went into overdrive, envisioning domestic life in a large white house atop a hill, in between

---

[9] A gay sexual act in which a couple enters into the traditional role of top and bottom, eventually switching positions during a single sexual encounter

Sally Fields' in *Brothers & Sisters* and Johanson's in real life. The Goode-Island manor would be three stories with a chimney. I want it separated from society so we'll have a field and stars, the scenery at the Anghel house, preferably not forty miles from town, though, more like fifteen. Under these delusions, I phoned Karen to talk me down from a cloud of imaginary romantic hysteria.

Directly following my explanation of *Not Another Gay Movie* and the characters Derek says reminds him of me and himself: "He loves you!" She, the romantic novel connoisseur, deemed.

"Uh... no, he doesn't. Not really," I countered, but Miss Asian Psychic refused to accept that.

"Yes, he does. And you're gonna get married and have a house on the hill and be a stay-at-home dad, and now all my friends will be happy and soon-to-be paired up and I can be happy because they're happy. Hey, Waldell, I'm you, now." Meanwhile, she has all this knowledge and still thinks my middle name is Thomas Abraham.

"What? No. It's this thing we have. We say and do things like that all the time and it means nothing."

"Are you sure about that?" she retorted.

"Well, there was that one time in the middle of last semester, he randomly called me at two or three a.m. and told me he was lying in a room full of half-naked men but wanted to talk to me. He told me he wanted to thank me whenever he won a Tony, which I thought was weird. Why would anyone call me in a roomful of half-naked men?" I had called and asked my longtime friend Pop about it, the only other man who sleeps with men that I really know, and he apologized and firmly stated there was no chance he would've called *me* while in a roomful of half-naked men. I'll never know Dare's motivations that night.

"That *is* weird."

"There's also the drunken texts he'd send me. One time he sent me, "you need to get your little ass fucked," but I don't think he meant specifically by him. It was quite descriptive. Besides, you can't really hold him accountable for what he says when he's drunk." When I asked Dare what he meant by the text the next day, he said it was because I'm too high-strung, and I informed him he shouldn't text me things like that because I'm more neurotic than high-strung, and it was only going to make me over analyze the suggestion.

"*Sure,* that's what he meant. And like you told me one time, drunken words are sober thoughts."

"Karen, that can't be true... now you have me thinking about my mother..."

"Let's not talk about your mother. We're talking about Derek!"

"Fine, but I don't think we can count bizarre drunken future Tony dreams as evidence for his love of Princess WaWa."

"He is the only guy in your life you're always talking to." That was true, except for Pop.

"He sent me an Ed Sheeran song the other day."

"It's Ed Sheeran. Can he make it any more obvious?" I was thinking of a reply to this, then I realized that our entire phone session had been terribly sidetracked by the bewildered Karen.

"You know, that's not even why I called. I'm not trying to question whether or not he has love for me 'cause I don't believe he has any. I called because at the slightest opportunity I decided I was becoming a stay-at-home dad with five kids and a husband. I wanted you to tell me why I was so willing to sacrifice everything I know about love and relationships for a chance to be Super Dad?"

"Because you and Derek belong together." Karen didn't help for shit.

A few days later, it was the weekend, meaning it was time for me to hang out with one of my closest friends in the world, Loretta Keep, a pleasant Derek distraction. We went to the movies, grabbed a bite to eat and consoled one another. *This is the End* shook my spirit. It was Whitney Houston. I told her of my woes and Karen's reactions, and Loretta gave me what I had expected at some rate to come from my primary ranting hotline:

"Derek Island? The guy who just looked at you?" Loretta was my date when I went to see one of the plays Dare directed at an actor's studio sort of production. Longwood. She added, "He didn't really seem like he wanted to embrace you in front of people. I feel like he's one of those guys who'll text you but wouldn't acknowledge you in front of his friends."

Thinking it over a while, that is what it sort of felt like. Derek wasn't in love with me, he didn't speak to me in front of his friends or whatever, and I was perfectly in tune with that before Loretta said anything. The bulk of our relationship transpired over text messages anyway.

A sashaying queen happened to be working the table not too far from us, and when he walked by, I worked up the courage to compliment him on his attention-grabbing strides. In the sweetest voice, he replied, "Thank you so much," exposing a dimpled smile and pearly white teeth. The twangy accent amplifying the ambiance.

"Perhaps he'd be perfect for Dare?" I offered, after the waiter had left to attend to his tables. Quickly, I realized it could never work. "Never mind, he's too mean."

"Who? That guy?" Loretta asked, stumped.

"No, Derek." I'm not saying he's evil, considering he's one of my favorite people in the world, but if Miss America sat down with the Queen of England, I'm sure the smiling size zero would leave crying, grab a bucket of fried chicken, and defenestrate herself. Unless that Miss America is Vanessa Williams before or after her infamous Playboy scandal. I'm sure that encounter would result in a verbally aggressive bitch-off, ending in a draw. I'm Derek's Vanessa Williams, and there's no need for another one in his life. Or I will take that bitch out. That bitch is going the fuck down!

Since catching dinner with Loretta, my thoughts of Derek had been manageable and I could reject the disillusioned notion of love that coursed through my brain. I refocused my energy on loading episodes of *Dawson's Creek* via Netflix. For a spell, I convinced myself I was perfectly fine again and only just a little sad.

As it happens, I wasn't expecting Derek to ask me to send him *Queen Called Bitch*, or what I had written of it thus far. He did, and complying to his wishes, I sent him the first ten chapters, believing that he would skim, reading only portions he'd like, or entirely never getting around to reading it at all, just as Pop had failed to do with anything I've sent him over the years. Imagine my surprise when I woke up the very next afternoon to a text from Derek asking, "Where have I been?" He further pushed, "I tell you everything. I consider you one of my best friends and knew barely any of what I read. I thought I was the closest thing to a man in your life. Apparently not."

I explained to him no one knew, that I hadn't had things to tell like I had a boyfriend or a life-changing theater experience, but that my mother was an alcoholic and it isn't the easiest topic to brace, he told me he was the closest thing to Blaine—the perfectly dapper homo from *Glee*—I had and it made him sad that he'd told me all his troubles and I couldn't do the same for him. He told me I should let him care, that he really wants to.

That could've been it. Those might have been the very words that persuaded me to love him forever. I need someone as well as I need them to care, and I would love for it to be Derek. I already love him, I know it. I want to sleep next to him and hold his hand in public. I want to kiss him whenever I feel like it... to feel his lips intertwined with mine might as well be God's touch of intimacy. I wish my first kiss had been Derek, had been with someone I loved and longed for. I yearn to wake up with him beside me and feel the warmth of his body and the rhythm of his heartbeat. I want us to love each other like they do in the movies. I want to be his Jack, only with him never letting go. I wanna touch the sky with him lifting me up, enabling me to, and I wanna make love, learning the raw meaning of what it actually feels like to do so. I want to live each day with him in springtime, and I want us to have at least 525,600 minutes together as we conquer every season of love. I want what everyone wants, though I foolishly thought I could escape it if I convinced myself I don't want something I need. And now, I don't even know if I'm in love with Derek or if I'm falling for the idea of sleeping next to a person rather than stuffed animals I named Reba and Loretta. I don't know, but wouldn't it be so very fine if I knew what it would be like to be held by him at least once?

I've tried my hardest to rebel against society's standard. A month after my stepmother's death, my father told me how he needed to be with someone, how it was instrumental to life and everyone longed for companionship. This was my father's great fault, and why he's often fallen so hard in his lifetime. I looked at him and said, "I'm just not like you and Mama and Diamond. I don't need to always be with someone, and I can find happiness within myself." That's true, but as Karen would be far too willing to note, I need to learn how to accept it from without as well.

I'm still not convinced of Derek's love for me. I don't think at night he pines for my touch, and I don't even think my feelings are permanent. I'm hoping they'll fade and I may bring myself back to reality instead of dreaming up foolish resolutions that'll never come to fruition, and I can stop wasting my life. In a few years, I do believe Derek and I will be at a wedding together. Contrary to what Karen believes, I will not be the other groom (bride, as she put it). I'm sure I'll be a groomsman, supporting my best friend Derek on the greatest night of his life. My only request is that he might visit me long after I've settled into a life with Karen, requiring a hearing aid and a miniature feline.

Twelve: Measuring Existence

I wish my mother had had an abortion. No bullshit. In the recesses of my mind, I ponder whether or not my existence has been beneficial to her, or substantial in any positive sense that I've been unable to recognize due to my own nearsighted self-deprecation. I regard myself as being pro-choice since it is the only rational conclusion any male can make, lacking the genitalia required to actually produce a living being (feel free to disagree). But I've wondered whether or not my mother made the wrong choice in having three children and should've ended the process at two. She'd have a considerably larger amount of finances at her disposal, she'd never have to suffer through the daily trauma of having a cross-dressing gay son, and she probably wouldn't have to work until her back ached so badly she required physical therapy. I cannot lay claim that I'm sure everything would've worked out better had I not existed, but I do concern myself with the notion that maybe her life wouldn't have been so bleak if only she made an appointment twenty years ago to remove the problem.

Approximately fourteen years ago when I was five, my mother and father were separated and my mother reentered the dating pool. This being years before PlentyofFish or OKCupid, Mother had met an English gentleman online who worked on a BMW lot in the UK and resided in a model home. He had a dog named Tie. Luckily, Niles Cook had to leave his pet overseas, much to the benefit of my canine-phobic mother.

As our matriarch primped in the mirror for hours, the three of us, Amethyst, Diamond, and I, watched as Mother prepared for her rendezvous with a real-life Frasier. My mother's always been a stunning woman and a master artist when it comes to her makeup; she could've given Da Vinci a tutorial so the Mona Lisa didn't end up with notorious bitch resting face.

Perfecting the final touches, my mother turned to her brood. "How do I look?" she asked, confident in her response.

Smiling, I knew I had the best line, "Mom, you look like an English whore." I beamed, certain that I nailed the question and my mom had absolutely no doubts I thought she was a queen. Need I remind you, I was *five*?

All eyes turned to me, and I felt the heat of my unwitting actions begin to invade my fleeting gaiety. I had made an uh-oh! My mother's eyes locked on mine, a vision of refined beauty. I took a breath and prepared to accept the weight of my actions even if I didn't completely understand the offense (usually the worse we ever got were a few whacks from a wire hanger, and I'm not making that up. My parents idolized Faye Dunaway as Joan Crawford). How pleased was I to find that my mother let out the loudest, most defining, uproariously resonating laughter I have ever heard in my life. The sound penetrated the barriers of my skin, and the other four eyes fixed in my direction wept tears of joy as my mother beelined to the phone to call her cousin, Lanetta, and discuss with her my uh-oh! *My* uh-oh! The shame and guilt of committing such crimes were no match for the validation and atonement that laughter bought me. And though I learned that I should never say that word again, especially regarding my mother, I learned it didn't mean exactly what I had thought it meant. My guess is it set the unconditional tone for our relationship: me saying things and her reacting to them, appropriately or not.

Senior year, I invited a friend to my house one day after school. I'd had a handful of friends over before, and my stepfather, who was always the hardest to convince, had given me the go-ahead when I called him at the last minute. He warned me my mother was off that day, indicating she had probably already begun drinking. That wasn't always the case. I decided to chance it, and Devin Shredder made the list of maybe five friends who've seen the inside of my home. Walking through the front door, Devin noticed a Woodbridge wine bottle lying atop the trashcan.

"How long have you had that?" asked Devin, her eyes wide and voice soaked with tender innocence.

"That's probably from this morning," I replied matter-of-factly. Granted, it was a rather large bottle, the largest made available at the local Food Lion. My mother didn't like to waste any time. Paraphrasing a rap song, she favored, "take it to the head" logic.

My mother, sensing a presence in the house lacking melanin, called me back into her room without ever meeting my red-haired and freckled friend. I don't think my mother's racist. After all, she would've married a pasty Brit with the surname Cook, but it didn't stop her from bringing up someone's race under the pretext of a drunken confrontation she was mostly having with herself. "Get her out of the house, now! Just go somewhere. You have no respect, and yet you bring this little white girl in my home," is what she told me. If I had been any wiser, I would've figured it was because she'd known she hasn't been her best self since that morning, and bringing someone over and not informing her, though I had tried to call at the last minute, was an invasion of privacy.

I reemerged from her room, trying to withhold laughter, when Devin asked me, "Oh my God, why are you laughing?" If she had been in my shoes, she would've seen the hilarity of the situation—or uncovered the actual truth—I laugh because it's better to experience the comedy in a situation, rather than the pain that pricks you in the thumb and begs for your tears.

We ended up walking across the street to Sheetz and grabbing a bite to eat. I told her that one time my mom threw one of her wine bottles at me and that's how I chipped my tooth. I think I made Devin cough up a mozzarella stick. It was not as funny a story as I had hoped. Actually, I chipped my tooth on the floor wrestling with Amethyst years before my mother's drinking became an issue. Devin and I sat outside in the humid high-80s temperature for a couple hours until her mom came to pick her up.

"I'm sorry for the circumstances," I offered. The situation of which was specifically left ambiguous. Thirty minutes after returning home, Mrs. Shredder, or Don as she prefers to be called, came back with snacks galore.

Eyes wide, "Hide them in your room. If you need anything, *anything,* do not hesitate to call me. I'll come get you *whenever.* I'll be there if you ask me to." Was that false wine-bottle-chipped-tooth story *that* convincing?

My relationship with Mother served as a great example for my fifteen-year-old cousin Jane, who likes to smoke and drink and do virtually anything aside from schoolwork. I was an enabler. I liked hearing her stories and telling people about them, up till she got into a huge argument with Amethyst the week of Wendy's death. Jane talks to people the way she wants to speak to them, most conspicuously to our grandmother, Aunt Darice, and Delsa, and no one says anything to her. At fifteen, she's the baby of the family. I feel it's time for her to grow up a bit.

Seeing her walk around the neighborhood smoking a cigarette infuriated me beyond my normal state of complacency. I took one from her, broke it, and threw it in the trash. Seeing her take out another one, I lost my control, which is something I *don't* do. There I was, the goof of the family, yelling in the middle of the street, crying with fury.

"What is it, Jane? Why do you keep doing this?" I barked, accepting my role as the surprise authoritative cousin. "You need to stop! It was cute then. It's not cute anymore!"

For the slightest fraction of a second, I saw the anger well in her eyes, and instead of releasing it, she began to cry, "Nobody cares about me." I never knew Jane had any weaknesses until then. I contested her argument with proof that I care. I try so hard not to care, and I was yelling at the top of my lungs in front of her world. That street in Newport News marked with at least four generations of familial pedigree.

She elaborated, "Ever since my mom met Kitch, she stopped caring about me." I didn't know what to say to this. Aunt Darice moved out of my grandmother's house to build a home with her man, leaving Jane with my grandmother five nights a week, having a room at Aunt Darice's new place for the weekend and breaks. I couldn't provide empathy for her current situation. My mother had always kept us with her no matter whom she'd been dating or was married to. I told her what I knew.

"Oh! You're still living your life for your mother. Honey, you can't do that. You have to live your life for you. Your parents have their own lives and you need yours. Your life should become your own, and you should have goals so your life has purpose." I offered what wasn't apparent to me. All those years, I was able to cope with my mom's addiction because God blessed me with the knowledge that my life is not according to anyone else but Her perfect plan, and God instilled enough faith and strength in me to know that my relationship with my mother was not defined by those moments in the wee hours of the morning when she'd engage incorrigible ramblings in an attempt to diminish those around her. I have a higher standard for myself. God has me protected, as trite and as awful as that sounds.

My relationship with my mother is a great deal of things, not one story or a few anecdotes, or not even one chapter as it turns out, and I am still learning that, unfolding that truth. Growing up, we make the mistake thinking our parents are one-dimensional and we're living in a 3-D world, or that who they are as people has a limited effect on who we inevitably become; we're wrong. Our parents are so much of who we are it's frightening to consider, and by the end of the day, you might not be able to sleep. Always remember that no matter how much bad you think you've absorbed and all the crap you fear you'll repeat, there is always that much good in contrast.

I have a memory of my mother buying a sort of Styrofoam football when I was in third grade. We went to the park and played catch since my father wasn't present. I'm sure we sucked and never played more than one time, but for a then nearly three hundred pound black woman, her effort was a true testament to any parent anywhere trying to make it work.

The nature of our relationship isn't *The Gilmore Girls*. Watching *The Anna Nicole Story* on Lifetime together, there was a scene in which Anna Nicole's son tries to aid his mother in losing weight. When they're running around a track, Anna protests her son's youthful energy and he comments that he likes to watch her suffer. My mom smacked me in the arm. When I asked her what I did to deserve that, her justification was, "It sounded like something you'd say..."

And it is. Given that I'm growing up my sentences are a lot more duplicitous than "You look like an English whore."

I'll never know how her life would be without me ever appearing in it. That's something that can't be backtracked or changed. I don't know why I consider the *would've been* as often as I do. The best I can do for me is to believe that my life has a purpose more than death so that I may achieve extraordinary things and fulfill the potential I am capable of. I'm learning that I have to allow myself to evolve into the person I'm going to become, and that I have to accept the things that I cannot change. My mother's life might have been more abundantly fruitful had she removed a developing fetus from her womb in 1993, but I'm here now and I've sort of grown accustomed to being alive. I have to push myself to burn the ashes of *would've been* and embrace an enticing promise my faith affords me, the thrilling proclamation of what *will be*.

Thirteen: One Word—Reba

Other than Jesus, Reba McEntire is my Alpha and Omega. That's not blasphemous. She set it up that way. Ever look toward the heavens and pray to God for an answer, a sign, a prophecy, or hell... forty virgins? Reba McEntire is my forty virgins. She's a direct symbol representing my security in the Lord. If I'm sitting at home and need a dramatic tune to act out, I play "Fancy." If I'm trying to relive the drama of the ever tragic 1980s AIDS Crisis, I play "She Thinks his Name is John." When I want to cry over my mother's alcoholism, I play "Because of You." If I should ever have to plan my own funeral, an obscure duet between her and Justin Timberlake would provide for an entirely fabulous, yet respectful, flaming home-going service. And what more could a southern precocious little pillow-biter like myself desire for such untimely events than a mellifluous voice humming in the background, making it the shindig of the season? I WILL BE REMEMBERED, BITCHES, but I digress.

Anytime I need a sign, a friend, a hug, something familiar and never changing to keep me together when it would be easier for me to fall apart, I look to God and She sends me Reba. Yes, I prayed and God sent a little gay black boy a fifty-something country-singing white woman. I would ask questions, but clearly She knows what the fuck She's doing. Keep it up, Christ, don't know what I'd do without you. (I'm sure as hell not becoming an Atheist. They get shaded more than Christians who take it up the butt.)

As a twelve-year-old boy, I naturally had an infatuation and unwavering affection for soap operas. The ill-fated *The Guiding Light* was my poison of choice, and I partook regularly. Undeterred by leaving school at three and generally missing the first ten to fifteen minutes, as I entered my grandmother's home roughly at 3:15 p.m. every day, I'd race to the kitchen, flip to CBS and engulf myself in Springfield, the land of sexual half-cousins, cancerous mothers, and gee, it looks like I need a third thing to complete the list. Oh well, I guess white people could be the third thing. Yes, there were *lots* of white people, kind of like a Republican convention.

Settled in my usual seat directly across from the television atop my grandmother's refrigerator (specifically placed, so we'd never make the mistake of communicating with one another as we ate), I eagerly turned to the untamed lives of Reva and her dysfunctional family. Doesn't every guy going through puberty find solace in TV dramas past their prime? Out of the blue, my cousin Jane suggested we check out this series advertised on Lifetime, which aired every day from 3:30 to 4. Having seen the trailers for said show and laughing out loud, I further protested, fearing that the regularity of my soap watching was at stake, and that's shit I don't play with. After slightly pleading with me, I changed the channel over to Lifetime, and like lightning in a bottle, I uncovered one of life's greatest treasures, *Reba,* a show so funny that even cynical in premise, divorced husband and teen pregnancy and all, I related to one of those kids whose once happy home has suddenly turned to shit. In life, I've attempted to find comedy in tough life situations as a defense mechanism, and this show taught me a lesson more important than my feeling abnormal for it—that whatever it is that allows me the ability to laugh when I come home from school when there's a cloud of smoke from my father's pot clogging the air vents in the house, is marketable and just maybe my meal ticket.

Falling in love with the show, it joined the ranks of *Roseanne, Who's the Boss, The Golden Girls, Gilmore Girls,* etc., shows that I'd seen every episode of and hold dear to my heart for getting me through rough days of being a bitter homo, and I haven't regretted missing half of that *Guiding Light* episode since. Besides, shit got weird once this guy died and his exes started boning. Is lesbianism really *that* convenient?

Later that evening, when Jane and I were bored in her room, she recommended we preview some of Ms. McEntire's musical work. I obliged without objection and it was like introducing crack to an ass. It was that bad. I'd pore through video after video, listening to the Queen of County Music! The capital letters make it an official title. I found the singer of my heart's songs, and life has never been the same. People say gays like to dramatize things, but seriously, I became weirdly invested in the then fifty-two-year-old's life. I knew when she was born, where she was born, that her first album was released in 1977 but her first number-one hit was in 1984 with "Can't Even Get the Blues," I knew she'd been married twice, her son, Shelby, is a year older than Amethyst—for that reason alone it'd make sense for them to marry. I knew her husband used to be her guitar player, they were both married to different people before they realized they were meant to be, that a plane crashed taking the lives of thirteen band members all on her payroll, that she was born March 28, 1955 and that she, like her father, used to be a steer roper and her siblings used to be in the Singing McEntires before she got her first solo gig singing the National Anthem at a rodeo show. She's the bomb and I knew it!

The first Reba CD I received as a gift was her then latest album, *Room to Breathe* for Christmas '06. Actually, I got it after Christmas because I was living with my father then, going home to my mother's for Christmas, and I'm pretty sure he wanted to leave some incentive for my return. And damn straight I did! I carried that CD everywhere. I would proudly blast it in my player at school. Living wild with Reba, I was such a fucking miscreant. Also, that was the year that I'd pretend talk on my prepaid phone my father bought me so people at school would think I had a life, friends, and wasn't lonely and weird. So yeah, I was mentally psychotic with my first Reba McEntire CD!

And then skip ahead five and a half years to Derek Island, promising he'd come to see me on a Thursday around twelve. I woke at ten, showered, dressed, and lay back in bed as I anticipated our lunch meeting. Karen had been pushing for us now for over a month and I pondered a magnificent encounter in my mind, hoping it'd manifest itself in a physical sense since this *was* Dare Fucking Island. That's seriously his middle name. We had been playfully corresponding, lightly and not-so-lightly flirting back and forth, taking our relationship to new heights. I let him read chapter eleven as per an impulse, egged on by the Asian, and a new gate in our friendship had been unlocked. We discussed sex, masturbation, penetration, and why Derek didn't find me sexy, much to my consternation. He told me I should be more open with my one-on-one sex practices, and release my fear of being sexually fluid in the ways of men. And that I'd be sexier if I thought of myself more sexually. He told me Princess WaWa was a force and I owned being my alter ego, but that should include a salacious pretense, and I was inclined to agree. Which is why when I went to a party after Dare revealed my innate inability to be seductive, I drank more than I ever had in my life, and dry-humped a physics major who sported a beard and fierce braid. I made an immeasurably bad decision for the first time in my life, and I don't regret any of the profanities I yelled that night when I wasn't getting enough attention.

I texted Derek regarding the situation and he seemed rather unfazed for the most part. I spent the better portion of a week at a girlfriend's house, texting Dareboy as I'd done every day for the past couple months, when he unloaded on me. We were reflecting on his thoughts, having watched the Lone Ranger:

Jul 26, 2013, 5:30 PM

Dare Island: *...armie hammer has a great voice.*
Me: *I don't need any more lover boys to fall in love with. I've reached my limit, lol*
Dare Island: *Oh, more than me?*
Me: *Yes, Dare. Everything always comes back to you.*
Dare Island: *Lol, I'm holding it over your head. I'm not really that self centered.*
Me: *That's what you think!*
Dare Island: *Wawa, I'd be perfectly okay if your rando bisexual reappeared and swept you away. It would bother me, but I would bounce back.*

Jul 26, 2013, 5:51 PM

Me: *What are talking about? Who's my rando bisexual? Any why would it bother you? Where did this come from. I'm confused. (Clearly typos are my life!)*
Dare Island: *That's what I think? I'm not self centered! And the guy that dry-humped you when you told him I said you weren't sexy.*

Jul 26, 2013, 6:01 PM

Me: *Are you drinking now? I still don't see why it'd bother you for one, I really don't think you're self centered for two, I was kidding, and for three are you feeling stressed because I really don't know where this is coming from. Like at all.*

Jul 26, 2013, 6:29 PM

Dare Island: *Lol I just don't get what you meant when you said that's what you think. I misdirected it or something. I'm sorry. And don't be silly. Because we have flier.*
Dare Island: *Because we have a connection.*
Me: *What does that even mean? I have a connection with my friend's dog but I don't think it'd bother me if she banged a stray.*
Dare Island: *Stop. You know what I'm saying. Would you be jealous if I started dating some guy?*

Jul 26, 2013, 6:47 PM

Me: *Insanely. But that's different. You know I have feelings for you.*
Dare Island: *I have some for you. Was that not clear?*

Me: *...I can't believe you have feelings for me. I never would've guessed. Honestly.*
Dare Island: *I've told you.*
ME: *When was this?*

Jul 26, 2013, 7:16 PM

Dare Island: Post your first confession. I feel for you too. (Referring to My Blaine)
Me: *That's fairly ambiguous. 'I kinda sorta like you, too' would've sufficed.*

That was it. That was our conversation about romantic feelings toward one another. We soon proceeded to decipher anxieties from stress and continued as we otherwise would, but it was out there. It was in the universe, and I was receptive to it. The next day I was alone in my friend's home, and upon informing Derek of that fact, he asked whether I stated it to allure him to her abode, and we'd make love on the floor. Telling him we'd go on endlessly and I'd be compelled to rip his clothes off, he noted he wouldn't last all night then and we moved on to topics closer to our repertoire, *American Horror Story* season one (his) and *Dawson's Creek* (mine).

Fittingly, months later as I waited for his arrival, my stomach flipped in knots. Not the kind that gives you the shits, the excruciatingly painful kind that you *wish* gave you the shits. Then at least you would know how to get the pain to pass. The knots grew tighter and tighter as he approached closer and closer, and the best advice actually came from Karen that time: "What are you nervous for? This is Derek." I remembered I had known him for three years, and he's a good friend of mine so I had nothing to worry about. The knots showed mercy, if only slightly. A blessing it was; I decided I was going to kiss him. I'm Princess WaWa in the flesh, how could I tell all my friends to go for it when I'd cower at my first opportunity for a love life. It was going to happen as soon as I saw him in his car. We'd be sitting down, I'd go straight for it to get it out of the way, and I wouldn't spend the entire time wondering whether I would or would not actually work up the nerve.

He called me as he came closer, asking for directions. He picked me up from home once to go see *Sparkle* a year prior, and he didn't remember exactly where I lived. He'd confided in me that he was worried that I'd make a giant declaration of love, such as standing in the doorway wearing only a robe and pulling a Mrs. Robinson, although he's three years my senior. The plan was to stand in the doorway wearing a robe and flash him as I stood there, only really wearing clothes underneath. Surprise! The problem was I couldn't give directions to my head seeing as I'm normally talking out of my ass. We agreed to meet at Walmart, a six-minute walk from my house. No robe, no clothed Mrs. Robinson.

I requested we meet in the Barbie aisle. I always felt safe there as a child and a semi-adult. It's sort of like my Mecca. Five times a day, I have to stop what I'm doing and pray toward the Barbie aisle in the nearest Walmart.

Subsequently, I began picking out the best outfit, something simple yet stylish: my tightest shirt, the pair of dark blue jeans Diamond gave me for luck, and no jewelry that would otherwise be used to impress someone. I was making a statement, presenting myself free of gaudy accessories for once in hopes that he would actually *see* me. Within the confines of the Barbie section, I received my last phone call from Mr. Island to date, telling me he could see me. I asked if he was sure, if he noticed my Mohawk. (In viewing all my photos he begged me to change my hair, but I didn't give a shit, I'm my own person, always.) I swung around and saw a tall, statuesque figure peering back at me, with gleaming white teeth and the bluest eyes, standing there perfectly, waiting for me. I hung up the phone and ran toward him an aisle over, and forgetting how big he was, I lifted on my tiptoes and wrapped my arms around him for too short a length of time as we inevitably had to pull away. He wore a black shirt, blue cardigan sweater, and regular-fit blue jeans; he looked fucking exquisite. I knew it wouldn't be the best idea to share a kiss by the five dollar DVD bin in Walmart with a guy I've seen for the first time in a year, thus it had to happen at the end of the meeting.

Conversation went as usual, only less eloquent and a bit more spiteful. Through text Derek had reprimanded me for "hate flirting" with him, like Mindy and Danny do on *The Mindy Project*. He threatened to post some embarrassing message I sent to his Facebook by screenshotting it, unless I apologized and called him sir. After about an hour of negotiation, I caved and he told me he had no idea how to screenshot and that I had gone soft.

We joked about his weight, Dare's six foot two and self-conscious about being two hundred pounds. He looks good at two hundred pounds. Hunched over he has a little tummy, and it's perfect and probably one of my favorite things. He bought me sushi. We laughed and sang to each other in the shop, and by the time we were finished devouring our lunch, he had time to kill before he was to meet up with his former frat buddies at Longwood. We drove around town and sang to each other. I stopped when "For Good" from *Wicked* began playing. Derek's moving to Kentucky for nine months in a couple weeks, right when I begin classes at Christopher Newport. He's leaving and is beginning a life there, and I can't even begin to contemplate how bittersweet it was having him sing me that song as we rode around town for the first and last time we'd ever have the chance to.

I sternly debated myself and reasoned not to kiss him. It would be the smart thing to do. He was leaving, I was leaving, and if I let myself love him, if I gave myself to him in the form of a kiss and he walked away from me, it could've been catastrophic and I don't know if I would've recovered. He told me he had a gift for me, and at a stoplight he pulled out *Dorian Gray* by Oscar Wilde.

"It's my favorite book. I've read it five times." He said. I don't know if it's the same for everyone else, but when a gay man parts with his favorite book, it's like he's giving you a piece of his heart. He's grown with the book, he loved the book, and he left it with me. I'm pretty sure it had a pulse of its own.

At last, I directed him back to my house and we prepared to say our goodbyes, I collected the book, looked in his face, told myself if I kissed him I'd ruin my life and everything I was to become. I embraced him one last time, taking in the smell of Derek before I opened and closed his car door and never looked back as I made my way to the side door of my house, through the kitchen, down the hall to my room, shut the door, laid in my bed, and sulked in loneliness, debating whether or not I should watch *Dawson's Creek* as a distraction from real life; it always seemed to work every other time. Too bad I didn't feel like moving or breathing, so I distracted myself with Facebook and Twitter until I received a call from Pop.

Pop had reconnected with a guy he dated a while back and really liked, but the guy had put the brakes on the relationship because things were moving too fast. The guy was used to sitting at home, playing video games and using his best friend as a crutch and an excuse to never have to find anyone else. He apologized for how things ended with Pop and wanted to have another go at things. Being the regional award-winning actor that I am, I told Pop that I was so happy for him, which is something that was genuinely true. I tried my best to conceal the pain in my voice at the non-happenings of the day.

"Oh my God, Waldell. Goodbye," Pop abruptly announced.

"Did I do something wrong?" I asked, curious as to why he'd be angry with my gaiety for his romantic trifles.

"You're just always so happy for me."

"Are you seriously upset because you have a friend who is always rooting for your happiness?" This is a real conversation, by the way.

"I don't know, it's just you're never happy for *yourself*."

"What do you mean I'm never happy for myself? I'm always happy for myself. I say I'm happy for you, but I'm really happy for me because I was right!"

"Hahaha, you're broken."

"What the fuck does that mean?"

"I don't have to explain myself to you!"

"Pop, I didn't say anything when you said I'm going to die old and alone, because like, I *am*. But this time you told me I'm broken? I think it's appropriate for you to follow up."

And of course he didn't. Of course on the day I didn't kiss Derek, or rather I didn't allow myself to kiss him, a friend calls me and tells me I'm broken because I'm happy his relationship is working out. I really didn't need to hear that at that point in time. Granted it was my fault, Pop didn't know I was even meeting with Derek, and I sure as hell wasn't going to tell him how much I loved Derek and still ran away from him, when he was literally staring me in the face. And maybe he didn't love me back, he hadn't tried to kiss me on his own accord, and I'm placing way too much power on one kiss that didn't happen.

The biggest hit of all happened when Derek stopped messaging me. We would text every day, throughout the course of the day. Not nonstop, but once he even messaged me how he didn't like *not* hearing from me. He disliked that he always had to text me first, so I started texting him first. He liked it when I sent him messages while he was sleeping since our sleep schedules are so different and he'd get them in the morning. When I left my phone unattended, he'd maybe send me three messages within an hour and commanded my attention. Now I don't get anything. He told me he was in a retreat and not conversing with anyone and, I don't know. I'm in my head, but he was a good friend of mine, and I loved him beyond any romance in a deep personal way, and now he's gone after I chose not to kiss him. I don't understand him and I can't stop thinking about him, replaying everything we've sent one another and everything we exchanged on the day that apparently ended it all.

Speaking with my girlfriend about it, Morgan Deathbox told me after he settles into his new living arrangements, I should get the address, hitchhike, and show up in Kentucky, preferably in the pouring rain and ask him to love me the way I need to be loved. I told her there's only one problem with that, it sounds like a romantic comedy and in those movies the girl always gets the guy. It's never the black man running off with Bradley Cooper.

I'm not the leading lady. I have long since made peace with that, evident in my lack of relationships from birth till now. No perfect guy is going to fight over me, or need me; I wasn't built to be loved, I was built to be successful, or at least that's what I tell myself. I realized I couldn't be fearless in my love life; I may as well take chances with my dreams, right?

Several days passed, I still hadn't heard from Dare aside from his Facebook updates (he watched Iylana Vanzant and he knows OWN is my thing), when I was invited to a party with the guy who dry-humped me. After a shot of something dark, mixed drinks and alcoholic Jenga, I walked over to him and stuck my tongue down his throat. It was relatively satisfying, as I went home and masturbated thinking about him. The next day I returned to his home with my friend, Blassidy, they started making out. He declared her a better kisser for not overly using her tongue like I did, and I was all for it. They have chemistry and I was just looking for a dick session. Oddly, in their presence I was more than okay without it. Like kissing him last night was a palate cleanser for my love life. I can go back to being content with my Snuggie and Netflix now that Dare is opting out of the picture, and I can only beg but so much for someone to talk to me.

Yep, braided dry hump guy was for my friend, and my life was once again for me. I could dream of having a job in New York, or maybe Boston, with an imaginative career, a large apartment and an eye for decorating. I could take a minute on braided guy's horribly puke-colored armchair as my friends were in the back room doing whatever they were doing in there, and see my life clearly without Dare for months. Although I still felt the urge to mention him every several minutes, I still had me.

Returning home after a hard day playing unnecessary wingman, I sat down at the kitchen table with my laptop, Lady Zorro, in front of me, and felt my chest sinking in. Dare didn't have to worry about that "rando bisexual" after all. No one wants me. That dude was only bi-curious anyway. It's not that I want dry hump guy, I honestly don't. I don't find him outrageously attractive, we would not work as a couple, he's a decent kisser (good enough to drunkenly masturbate to anyways). He's good for Blassidy and that makes me smile.

By *no one*, I mean Derek. He's still everyone to me. I went on Facebook and changed the status of our friendship from "close friends" to "acquaintances" so I wouldn't have to see his name three times a day when he posted about *American Horror Story*, Broadway, New York, Meryl Streep or something else Broadway and media related. I don't want to think about how that's not my role to play, that I was born to be single, that I am broken from reasons I'm not sure of and things I can't fix. I want to be happy. I want to accept what God has given me and excel at whatever it is I'm meant to produce under Her grace. I want to be fixed. As Jane Fonda said on an OWN special, "I want to be whole."

How am I supposed to put me back together if I have no fucking idea where the pieces went? And here I am, wounded and lost, pretending to be fine but hoping to be okay. In the silence of five a.m., I play an unreleased Reba song, and repeatedly listen to it until I can walk away with my "Head Held High." If I can play it enough times, I can believe in its philosophy, not showing any tears, dignity intact, leaving the situation stronger than when I came in. In it not mattering if he loved me back, if he'll never text me again, if three years of friendship is that disposable. When all else fails, my head's held high. I can't tell if it'd make a difference whether or not I ever find love, or if Derek's the one, if I don't have a one. I am due for a damn good life either way, and if I have to settle for great friends, a wonderful home, one or two adopted kids I've chosen to single parent and a meaningful career, so be it. There will always be something to get me through the dark nights or to make me feel warm when I fear my soul may give way to self-induced hypothermia, something to calm my nerves when I find Pop's prophetic statements to be true, and a spiritual reminder when I forget I am more okay than I know I am. I will always have *Reba*.

Fourteen: Cann

Cann Johanson has one of those souls that need other souls to survive. This isn't a unique trait in any fashion, except for that Cann suffers from a condition forbidding her to admit such verities. Her quiet spirit doesn't require thousands of responses, but a choice few to relate to her sense of isolated being. Yes, Cann suffers a phenomenal inner working that requires persistent, if not exhausting, interpersonal relations, forming a bond impenetrable to any outlying source.

Just kidding, that bitch called me Gaylord two years ago and I've never gotten over it.

The truth about Cann is that she is *not* Cann. She is Carol, or as I have known her, she has been. Carol wasn't always Cann, or in fact she was, if we're speaking technically. Metaphysically however, the two couldn't be more... similar. What I'm trying to say is, Carol is not Cann but Cann is Carol because I have a hard time with change and I don't like that my friend is going by a new name. Granted, Cann is more gender neutral but Carol is more familiar, and if I'm being immature it's acceptable because I'm writing this fucking story and it goes as I want it to. Okay, I'm being a brat and confusing myself now, so yeah, this is just like high school.

Carol and I had long since been friends when Johanson drove us home from a tame high school party well supervised by adults (they were the only parties we were ever invited to), and Carol started talking shit about her father. I know this is an odd place to begin this particular narrative; it proved to be more insightful than I originally assumed. After all, talking smack about one's father is simply a rite of passage for everyone except Karen.

"God, he's such a fucking asshole!" Carol fumed, her mother's mouth agape at such an impromptu and impassioned declaration.

"Carol! What's wrong with you?" She demanded.

"I never talk about this and you know I don't. He's never there for me. He doesn't do anything. He can't keep a job. I just fucking *hate* him." Carol and her mother's banter always stretched the observer's imagination when it came to passable language in a familial setting. Generally though, nobody really gave a fuck.

I spoke up. "It's okay, I understand. My father isn't exactly the greatest either." Thinking back on it, I should've gone with the "Our dads should go bowling," line from *The Breakfast Club*. It was the exact same sentiment, not to say that this work is derivative in any way because it's not! It's completely original as it's the first coming-of-age story ever told. I'm so different, just like everyone else.

Anyway, Carol continued unleashing her obviously pent-up frustrations into my listening ear, no matter how unsolicited the ranting pontification may have been. I understood. I have been there. I didn't ask any questions, just received what she was willing to tell me. The point of the ordeal being, having someone to tell your issues to as you want to present them, and not having an interrogation of every negative feeling you've ever had concerning half the origin of your chromosomal heritage.

"Carol, he is still your father," Johanson protested once or twice. Carol's argument continued for maybe ten to fifteen minutes. I took note of how contrary the scene was from my patriarchal rants with *my* mother. She yells and curses his existence while I resist the urge to remind her *she chose him to have children with, not me!* Johanson actively chose to maintain Carol's respect for her father, not something every custodial parent does for their noncustodial counterpart.

"I need to say this, you know I do." Johanson wasn't really trying to get Carol to stop talking, but to monitor or censor her language, the first time I ever heard Johanson implore such a tactic. Johanson drove back to the tiny duplex apartment I lived in with my mom and stepdad; I told Carol goodnight, and that was the last I heard of her father for a fortnight. (Not really. I wanted to use that word.)

After our school play, *Property Rites,* had ceased production that year, Carol, through her mother's connections, was cast in Longwood University's *The Grapes of Wrath*. I'm sure she was all too eager to step into an acting experience that wouldn't begrudge her for wanting to visit her father in the hospital, or warn me that if I didn't play a character gay enough our director was going to take a flagpole and shove it up my a**.[10] High school theater under Ms. Fast sure brings back many memories.

Through a miracle of sorts, Longwood University needed a young black actor cast in a small part with six lines in the denouement. Carol instinctively thought of me. In Mr. Jackson's class, the school's far superior and boisterous English instructor, she told me if I joined she could give me rides, and that she missed hanging out with me. Also, there were gays there. Just maybe three: one who says he isn't but clearly is—the director told him to walk like a man on several occasions, and one extremely weird kid who was to play my father, and another guy who was unimportant. The former two became my best friends.

Upon making my debut, I saw a lean, six-foot, smiling African-American sporting an afro walk past me to dispose of something in a nearby trashcan. He was grinning awfully wide, and his eyes were nearly popping out of an engorged head, which was probably the reason for 90 percent of his body fat, given that he had a twiglike frame. His mere image struck me as one of an individual, and I had never seen a person that gay before in *real* life. He was gayer than anyone on television, he was gayer than anyone on the street, he was gayer than any character I had to be for Fast's satisfaction, and he was just gay enough for me, and that is how I met ShaVaughn "Pop" Peterson. The other homo was Dare, and I haven't slept with either one of them. What kind of gay am I?

Carol and I bonded behind the scenes in the dressing rooms before the show. We'd make each other laugh, and talk about our day—typical high school drama. She secretly had a boyfriend until I discovered a classmate jacked him off out of pity while he and Carol were supposedly "dating." That incident ended one of two of her flighty high school romances. The second and last came and went during senior year, and that was so tragic George Bush ignored it, and personally thanked FIMA for their involvement.

She was also as extremely temperamental as I was annoying. I just am, I've learned to cope. We could be having a splendid time kicking up our heels, then one minute later she'd explain she needed her space and I'd give it to her, only for a minute until she'd decide to speak to me again.

---

[10] The only time Fast ever censored herself.

There wasn't much I understood about her, but when someone needs space you give them space. It's the least you can do, unless you're planning on flying into their brain and fix all their problems. We hugged each other twice, aberrantly, as per my initiation. I felt like I forced her to do something she didn't really want to do and we didn't talk about it after that.

Her father came to pick us up several times. He was charming. He was a cynical, short, fat man, who I have only ever seen standing once. He gave me rides so I didn't complain. Carol's conversation with him seemed contrived and calculated. She didn't say too much, nor did she say much in the way of substance. I'd categorize their relationship as polite when possible, though to my knowledge he'd make even that difficult. He drove me to practice on his own without Carol one time; he gets points for that.

The bulk of our *Grapes* practices took place during the middle of winter. It was nice because we had gotten the biggest snowstorm we had in six years and missed a fortnight of school. We didn't have to read *Candide* or write any current event articles, we just had to rehearse *Grapes* until opening day. Ending each rehearsal, we'd go outside waiting for Johanson, dancing and singing while freezing our asses off. The closer to opening night, the more hectic our schedules became. We'd leave Longwood sometime around midnight, allotting the night to be ours alone. Just mine, Carol's, and the alternative theater kids of Longwood.

Sooner or later, opening night came and we received mixed reviews. I received negative ones. My emoting was great. My pronunciation was irrefutably horrendous. I will note that after being told when I asked for soup or milk in my penultimate line, it sounded like "super milk," further demonstrated by the director, the famed Pamela Arkin, saying, "'Soup or milk' not 'super milk'" and grabbing her boob to aid the demonstration, I cleaned up my enunciation real quick.

A week into our show, Prince Edward had to reopen its doors and it was time for our school to take a field trip to see the show, as they did with a number of Longwood plays. I had my shit together that performance. A former cast member from *Property Rites* asked one of the actors about behind-the-scene flubs, and the gorgeous blond who played Tom pointedly called me out on super milk. God, I cannot get the image of that aged tit out of my head. Still, Pamela Arkin is a goddamn national treasure. Fight me.

The next day, I rode the bus to school and noticed all the snow melting away, and similarly so had my time backstage at Longwood. Carol and I had won something, those days and in those hours staring at Pop and his friend Olivia, the eeriest mirror of ourselves only taller, waiting for our time to go on backstage. We didn't need to cry or hug, share a tampon or become blood sisters or anything when it was all over. We knew we had something special then, and it was rare if only to us.

Granted, we saw each other frequently, going to movies and bumming around Carol's home with Karen, but nothing was ever quite like us slumming it with the college kids as high school sophomores. We were so fucking cool.

Our friendship progressed in a number of ways, including the physical sense. We were no strangers to violence, with mostly me being the primary physical aggressor, not to say she never asked for it.

One of the times I had come over, it was just me, her and Karen congregating around her kitchen table. We were laughing and shooting the shit when I chose to tell them about Jason, the cute guy who worked in the movie theater and always flirted with me and once took me to the movies as his compensated guest.

"When we got in his car, he told me he was bisexual." A sexuality worthy of all the 2007 Jojo I found on his iPod. "Then, two days later we spoke on the phone and he told me he was straight. Which sucks because now I'm just confused."

Then Carol, with her snarky know it all attitude belted, "Wah wah, my boyfriend pretended to be straight to get away from me."

Karen and I stared at her. "Wow, that's mean," spoke the ambassador for human rights. I was silent and perplexed, I didn't say anything and allowed several beats to pass before I picked up the plastic fork and stabbed the future carpet muncher in the arm. Unfortunately, the fork lacked the strength necessary to break skin, her skin actually broke the prong. No words were spoken, but I got my point across. #ThugLife. No one fucks with an angry gay. We still laugh about it today. Or I laugh as she remembers the pain. "Why so serious?"

Oh, and that one time she called me "Gaylord," she knew exactly what she was doing. I think knives were involved.

Over the years, our relationship took on a much more serious tone when Carol elaborated on her paternal issues. I was spending time with a mutual friend, and she revealed to me that Carol's father was gay. Carol wasn't present at the time. I was obligated to keep that revelation in the back of my mind; I sort of had to un-hear it if that was possible. That information was so private and something Carol obviously kept from me; it was the personable thing to do.

In her living room a few days later, the two of us by ourselves, she referenced her father's sexuality and I further inquired, with her response being, "Oh, I haven't told you?" It turns out her father's coming out wasn't only the end of her parents' twenty-year marriage, but also his career, and literally, his sanity. While Johanson was cleaning out his things she found a hidden stash of Bette Midler albums, tucked away like it was porn. Tragic story, priceless moment.

The snarky bitch retreated inside an actual person for a few seconds, and our spiteful retorts ceased as she told of an area of her life that still festers like an open, oozing wound. Carol's eyes were always deceptive when it came to reflecting what she was actually feeling inside, but no one could deny the overwhelmingly melancholy air of a friend confiding in another about the intensity of her father's mental illness and inability to fully accept who he is.

Assured, she avoided my eyes. "My father should take responsibility for his actions. In large part society and its innate homophobic social expectations played a part in the demise of a once reliable family man. He was an artist. In the very least, he once was competent."

Mouth shut, my eyes did l the talking.

Exhaling raggedly, "If society didn't force its mentality onto my family, maybe I could've ended up with three dads and a mom, instead of a mom and half a man who continually battles trying to be a father, or even a person." I discovered that those horrors haunted Carol every day of her life, and her childhood was forever marred by principles of a society that doesn't have a fucking clue. She deserves more than that.

I'd like to think that Karen and I helped, or at least aided her in not feeling so lonely. The Friday nights we were together were the best. We'd end up doing the same things pretty much every Friday night. In school, we weren't apt to be involved in drama, so when someone was thrown through a window in the middle of the hallway, we weren't privy to endless details regarding the live-action defenestration, except that it happened and there was excessive amounts of blood. Slip on *that* on your way to second period.

We watched television, sat through half of *Pulp Fiction*—I don't know why that movie's a thing. We ate chocolate, read Tarot cards, and once tried to make a can of Diet Coke explode on Carol's front porch, to my objection, believing the house would blow up and Johanson would come home from her party to blame me. They *knew* she would. We must've gotten the chemistry lesson wrong because all we ended up doing was throwing the can outside and burying the failed explosive in the snow.[11]

On a typical Friday after school let out, we'd just eaten pizza and Carol was forced to pause *Supernatural* when Karen squealed, "Oh my God, it's snowing!" She ran outside decked out in her matching purple hat, gloves, and scarf, and I followed in my scarf and I think Carol came out wearing a tank top and sweats. We ended up running around in circles singing Katy Perry's "Teenage Dream" aloud at the top of our lungs, never missing a beat as perfect snow crystals graced our surroundings, brushed against our shoulders, and settled betwixt our hair and on the ground. It was something out of a John Hughes movie or one of its many later homages. Everything about that night was perfect, and what cements that moment as one of my most cherished, is that we were all together, we all really loved each other, and that, unequivocally, was enough. Yes, we talked about boys and our dreams, realizing how magical and surreal the experience must've been. It was the scene from a thousand novels and the poetry of every rhyme and an ode to the greatest relationships I've ever had in high school, and thus far in life. It was intimate, it was once in a lifetime, it was a fairy tale, it was a dream, it was beautiful, and it was like no other moment ever on this Earth.

Every few months, Johanson would host an art exhibit at the Longwood Center for Visual Arts. They were swanky affairs, and Johanson prepared all the information per painting; she organized a gala mainly to schmooze with fundraisers, and managed, tirelessly, to actually make the event enjoyable. Mostly, I came for the food. Carol would drag me along, sort of as arm candy, and her mom's colleagues would frequently stop her, inquiring about school, or to congratulate Carol on her latest success or whatever. Carol was regularly featured in the local paper winning awards at the regional and state levels, predominantly for her writing abilities. I enjoyed attending such a refined shindig, again mostly for the food.

---

[11] That may or may not have actually ever happened. I've been sworn to a lifetime of secrecy. Only Olivia Pope could crack me now.

After three or four of these gatherings, several of the art patrons had come to recognize me. Carol told me when we were alone; they assumed I was her girlfriend. Not female friend, but that we were partners. Evidently, I was that androgynous in high school. At least they had gotten used to seeing me, and I no longer seemed like that bizarre kid always hanging around for no reason.

Senior year, they had no trouble placing me as soon as they saw me, nor did they hesitate to speak directly to me without trying to figure out who the fuck I was. I made a Facebook post announcing that I'd been accepted to Howard University, and either Johanson saw it or Carol told her mom, because Johanson's colleagues were eating that shit up. A black college that they knew was prestigious that was also safe for white people happened to be well within their comfort zone. They urged me to go, practically pushed me through the doors, but I wanted to go to Emerson. Fancy rich white people be damned. In the end, *I* was damned; I didn't end up attending either school.

Retrospectively, I see how I was taken in by Carol's family. I was new in eighth grade, no friends or connections or people in my life here, and there I was being interrogated about my future college plans as if I was Johanson's extremely tan son. Things change considerably over four years.

There were many things that happened senior year. After vacationing with my father's family in Newport News over Christmas break, I returned home and left for Carol's house that same evening to spend New Year's. Shuffling me into the kitchen where we'd spent the prior four years of our friendship, she looked me directly in the eyes, and lacking much prelude, she enlightened my perception of her sexuality.

"I'm bisexual," she imparted with a smile containing the awkwardness of uncertain fortitude.

I glanced toward the heavens with shaking fists, screeching in angst, *"I meant a boy!"* I had been praying to God for a gay friend to come in my life, not someone I'd necessarily become an item with, simply someone who understood where I was queerly coming from. And He gave me Carol.

"And, you aren't allowed to become an angry lesbian!" Johanson called from the background, preparing to bake us homemade nachos to celebrate the joyous occasion.

It didn't automatically register with me. I didn't instantaneously replay the entirety of our friendship; I did come to terms with how she identified sexually. I could recall several months back on Halloween when we watched *Hedwig and the Angry Inch* and Carol mentioned she thought Hedwig was hot. I noted that Hedwig made a pretty girl, and while she was trans, there was nothing manly about John Cameron Mitchell's signature creation. Like all transwomen, Hedwig was just a woman. There was also the first day we'd ever hung out, she said that she wanted to kiss a girl because that's something she thought she should do. I guess it's something she'd more than enjoy doing now. We watched John Waters' *Female Trouble* twice that night, once with commentary, and she scared the shit out of me when I went to steal her Jesus-shaped angel chocolate, causing her to scream like hell. That was her coming out party.

"You cannot wear flannel or be misogynist," Her mother warned.

"Why would I be misogynist?" Countered the newborn lesbo.

"You cannot hate men!"

"You mean misandry?"

"Oh, whatever!" And I have to say, a year and a half later, Cann has been fraudulent on both accounts. In the morning, we toasted the New Year with mimosas before Carol's mom drove me home.

As Karen sees it, that's when things began to change. Before January in senior year, we were the three non-slutty amigos, and Karen seems to think the fact that Carol told me and didn't say anything to her drove a wedge between us. I urged Carol to come out to her because I couldn't keep a secret, least of all from Karen, but she just didn't feel comfortable for whatever reason. Disclosing that information to Karen didn't make sense to her. Maybe because they were awfully close and have seen one another naked regularly, which would make coming out even more of a pain. She hadn't the slightest romantic feelings toward Karen at all. Not that Karen cared anyway. Since then, Karen's felt distant from her best friend.

The last remarkable day the three of us spent together senior year was during the first semester of high school after seeing *Don't be Afraid of the Dark*. We ran around outside of Farmville's lone movie theater, and I ended up dancing on a table by the abandoned Quiznos to Tina Turner's "Proud Mary" before one of Johanson's protégés appeared to take us home. Our threesome then morphed into a more often twosome. Carol and I would get sushi, then we'd get in line for the movies; our typical dialogue mirroring the high regard with which we care for one another:

"Hold on, I have my wallet in here somewhere," I'd say, searching my oversized tote bag for a small change purse I stuffed in along with necessities like scissors and extra toothpaste.

"That's why you should only carry a wallet, cell phone, and house keys. Everything on command."

"You know what Carol... suck a dick and die," I puffed, still searching for the eight dollars I needed.

"Really, in that order?" She pushed like she always did.

"Oh, so you want to die first? 'Cause then you'll be sucking Satan's rusty cock. One for The Muppets, please!" Can I just say, that comeback was legendary. One of our top Carol and Waldell moments, next to Carol mocking a terrible play I'd written based off of Faith Hill's "Stealing Kisses," and the time I was so overcome with grief when Whitney Houston died. I accidentally whacked Carol in the face and broke her glasses. That wasn't deliberate. I kept asking for space and she wanted to annoy me - our usual bit, we take turns. Spatial Reasoning issues. Then she went all Gloria Steinem on us.

At Karen's Fourth of July party sophomore year, Johnny Gabble and I found a spot secluded from everyone else, on a church stoop where we watched the fireworks and spoke about our dreams. Junior year Carol joined us, and senior year I was alone. I didn't mind. Sometimes there are moments that deserve to be more personal than you would allow them to be. That's how people grow.

The second to the very last time I ever went over to Carol's that year she told me she considered suicide. She thought about it one day about a month before telling me. She thought about running a bath, or rather for more poetic effect, jumping into the creek not too far down from her house and ending everything. She decided against it, thankfully. I knew I couldn't stop her, that if the thought of breaking Johanson's heart couldn't prevent those thoughts, there wasn't anything I could do to rectify her grievances.

I asked Carol that if she ever chose to go through with one of those horrid decisions, that she at least text me goodbye. I know when someone makes that decision there is little to anything anyone can do to prevent them from taking their own lives. She assured me it'd never get that bad, that she had spoken to her therapist about it and everything was going to be okay, that she was feeling so very trapped the day she contemplated it, that things were better now. I hoped she would be, if only for her mother's sake. Johanson wouldn't recover, *ever*. Carol lived another day, another year and a half more so far, and things are looking good.

Graduation went as expected. Karen cried, Carol was salutatorian, and I was there making sure opposing sides of my familial spectrum didn't come to unnecessary and overwrought blows revisiting the past. Mother wore an outfit I picked out, leaving me feeling like a winner.

Two months later, Carol was off to Massachusetts to attend Smith. I left for Newport News, and Karen for Christopher Newport University—unbeknownst to me, five minutes from where my father and Wendy lived. We left the same day. I've seen Carol twice since then. Once when I went to visit her at Smith via my overly generous Cousin Mike, and once over Christmas break.

She told me her father finally admitted to his homosexual desires and that they may have an honest relationship developing. Johanson flew around the United States, writing an article analyzing academic presidents and the politics in running prestigious universities, spending a plethora of time interviewing several of the nation's most distinguished scholastic intellectuals. Johanson did not visit Christopher Newport University. Carol has had several sexual experiences, some coming pretty close to orgasmic proportions. She cut her hair and appears to go out more nights than she stays in, and appears like she's in the right place at the right time for herself. We were chatting on Facebook one day when I received a message from her, long after she dropped her last name to go by Johanson's maiden name, which, just to clear things up, is actually Johanson. Katie is her mom's first name:

May 7, 2013 8:31 PM

Carol: *Thought I should let you know that I'm changing my name soon to something more gender ambiguous.*
Me: *Legitimately changing it?*

This felt like an overhaul to me.

Carol: *Informally for now, but I think eventually legally. It's a tie between "Cann" and "Case" right now.*

Me: *Haha, this is what Massachusetts does to you. So, not only are you not returning at all to Farmville (possibly ever) you've also changed your last name and now reconsidering your first. Who are you?*

Carol: *God, I don't even know. I might come back next year for break and no one will recognize me. Which I kind of like, to be honest. I just hate the gender binary and have never felt right being so feminine. Not to say I'm a transman though. I have zero interest in surgeries, hormones, or male pronouns.*

Me: *Okay, so at least there's that to hold on to. The gender binary is, and has always been fucked up, so I support you. But again I have to ask, who are you? What next, are you going to join an alt band called The Period Munchers or something? Maybe drum for a Tegan & Sara cover band?*

Carol: *If only I had any musical ability whatsoever I totally would. Ugh, I hope you get to go to Hampshire[12] then we could fuck up straight society together.*

That's the last we had of the conversation since she officially decided to the change her name. She's Cann, now.

I hadn't wanted to dwell on that or give her the third degree regarding her decision, making her think I didn't support her or want her to express herself in the most natural way she felt, but she was Carol to me. Always Carol, so it scared me when she became Cann. One late night I was online when I saw Lona, the best friend Carol acquired while attending Smith and bonding over an oddly intense crush they both had on their film professor, was online.

May 9, 2013 3:54 AM

Me: *Why the hell are you awake?*

I hoped I wouldn't simply be ignored as a friend of a friend she only interacted with once.

---

[12] My cousin, who I met at a funeral when I was eighteen, has a scholarship there in his name.

Lona: *paper for none other than the fabled Jen Malkowski*

That was the professor Cann was always talking about, the one with the Justin Bieber haircut and a Cracker Barrel obsession. We discussed intense lesbian sexual acts until I addressed the reason for messaging.

Me: *So, what is this Case Johanson?*
Lona: *i think, last i checked, 'Cann' was the frontrunner*
Me: *Damn. Really? I guess it is more... idk, obscure? Anyways. How do you feel about this?*
Lona: *meh, her name, her rules. to a certain extent i understand the need she feels to not associate herself so strongly with one particular gender. also, i imagine it's a pretty big "fuck you" to her dad, since her name is like, the one form of ~her identity~ that he helped bestow upon her, i guess. besides that good ol' family gayness he passed down*

She's more evolved than I am.

Me: *Yeah, I get the last name thing, at least that makes the most sense to me, but it's the first name thing that's throwing me off. Maybe I'm reading too much into this, but it's weird when your friend has a change of identity. You know, are they still the same person? But then again that's dumb because of course they are! But then again they're not. They've grown, they've adapted in an honest and declarative way. They're different than before, but they're still the same. I'm rambling, this is what I do, but I'm asking because I'm hoping you have more experience with this than I do. How should I go about approaching the situation?* That's me, not long winded at all.
Lona: *it's very insightful rambling, if that helps. i don't know if it's a matter of experience or whathaveyou, it's honestly probably that I've just been in closer physical proximity to Carol for the past few months. i think that it's just another step for her to come into her own, really. to me, it's just kind of like she's picking a nickname at an older age than most people usually do—if she doesn't feel as personally linked to her current name than she used to, i guess i don't really see why she shouldn't take the initiative to change that for herself. i guess, instead of a change, i would see it as a development. does that make any sense? i am half-asleep.*

I appreciated her willingness to try even when I was keeping her from a worthy slumber.

Then this happened.

++
++
++
++
++
+++++++++++++++++++++

Still from Lona. Maybe that was the lesbian way of emphasizing a point.

Me: *Yes. That makes a lot of sense, and makes me feel better, actually. You know when you grow up you lose friends or they change and evolve into different people. Some you lose and some you keep. I guess my main concern is just losing Carol because I always figured I knew who she was, for the most part anyways. The whole act of separating a new name from a new person clarifies things. Thanks, you've really cleared shit up and made me feel better. I hope you have a good night, Lona. And if you ever need anything, talk to Carol's mom because I probably couldn't help you with shit.*

Lona: *sat on the keyboard dude my bad*

Lipstick lesbians are imperfect too, it turns out.

Me: *Haha, no problem. Night night!*

Lona: *also, bahahahaha! I'm glad i could help, for real!!! in KJ we trust.*

The Katie Johanson is God reference was gold. We said good night, and I've been trying to accustom my tongue to forming Cann instead of Carol when I need to tell the less informed public of one of my best friend's queer pursuits.

Sometimes, I think I'm having a hard time accepting this new person into my life, then I think about Karen, distanced from her best friend for a year because of some trivial secret, and then I remember what I have is not that bad at all. What if she had desired a sex change, or rejected her assigned gender? Would that have made a difference? Again, these are trivial matters, though frankly, they don't seem as such. As you grow and change you have to remember what's really important in life, to really look to people beyond the name they're given or change for themselves, to who they are deeper than that, deeper than sex or gender or anything else people otherwise have little to no control over whatsoever when they were given these labels. Maybe that's what Cann was accomplishing by choosing a gender neutral name? Now as her friend I have to consider her more for her intelligence and human condition other than anything else. I would like to think that for the most part I have done this, but judging from the way I reacted when she decided her name was too feminine, there's always room for improvement.

At Karen's most recent Fourth of July party, I went with a friend I grew closer with after starting college, Loretta Keep. She's weird around people she hasn't spoken to in a while, so she instructed me at this party that I couldn't leave her side. We scurried off to my spot on the church stoop. I told her that it was the best place to watch the fireworks, unknowingly in the danger zone. I told her that we were good, I've sat there for three years already and we were okay. I failed to realize they moved the physical position of the actual fireworks to maybe one hundred feet north of the church, and I clung to Loretta praying that the Jesus idol out front would protect us. Once we were in no imminent danger, we lay on our backs watching the explosives light up the sky, like an incandescent spider crawling through arching rainbows. I looked at Loretta and a pang of sadness swept through the moment, and I told her not to take offense, that I was overjoyed to be there with her, but that I missed Carol.

Back at Karen's house around midnight, ten of us remained, sitting around and talking, when I had to step away to the computer in order to forward Dare and Karen my latest copies of *Queen Called Bitch*. Peering at the eclectic bunch, I remembered how Carol and I would've hated how scenic and Norman Rockwell the scene played out. I had to choke back tears, my heart was being squeezed by memories I never knew were so pertinent, until they were years apart, and we could never go back because that's not how life works.

No more screaming bitch fits in public or viewing faux-wrestling matches in the middle school gym, watching art films on her mother's couch or singing loudly at the top of our lungs watching *Princess and the Frog* while I hogged the Ben & Jerry's all night. Now all that is left is the future, and as much as I don't want to admit it, there is no more Carol. There is no more Karen or Waldell either, for that matter. Not as we were. Not all of that naïve dreaming has survived from then until today. There's no more *Supernatural* episodes we watch over and over together, or heart attacks I can give Johanson when I try to take excess jam from restaurants forcing her to exclaim, "They are not free samples, they are individual servings." I've antagonized her enough. She screamed it across the table at Galaxy Diner, something I assume she seldom does when she and Cann are dining out as a duo.

I don't know. I suppose what this is really about is my fear of growing up, and not of letting people go because I won't. I have to accept that she's Cann and I'm not who I used to be, nor is the Asian. Currently, we're different and that's how you deal with the changes life thrusts upon you, and it is an act necessary for survival, as the three of us have exceptional futures lying ahead. I don't mind having memories like that time I suggested Cann acquaint herself with Satan's flamingly corroded appendage. Or how they sting.

P.S. Editing this, I just realized Cann and I were Prince Edward's Ambiguously Gay Duo.

Fifteen: Fucking Stupid

Derek met someone else in Kentucky. Things didn't work out between them. He messaged me, *you got your wish. He friendzoned me lol.* I just wish I wasn't so fucking stupid. I hate that I'm human. I hate when I can no longer pretend that I'm not. I hate that I thought he knew me when he didn't know me at all. I wanted him to be happy, why couldn't he just see that. I hate that he was my best friend, and I hate that I've been listening to sad Kellie Pickler songs because they're cathartic. I wish I was as fabulous as I claim to be. I wish my character was as incorrigible as my emotions are. I pray to be superhuman with a powerful mind and body, and even still an imperishable heart because I feel like that's the part of me that folds the most quickly. I long to not be myself, to reflect the force I've framed myself to be. And I wish my heart didn't feel like death, so I may reclaim my attention and reflect it back toward the righteous origin of its pursuits, myself.

Sixteen: Sex...Or Not?

It had to happen eventually. It wasn't the greatest experience; it wasn't the worst, either. It took a considerable amount of chutzpah in order to take such an engorged tension forcing its way through my body. I had to open up and accept the pain as I knew it was the only way to encourage mental and physical relief, culminating in a stimulating and vigorous sense of pleasure. Silently, within my own grief, I trembled. It was going to happen, my heart rapidly pounding within its suddenly fragile cage. I wanted to run, I wanted to hide behind an encompassing blockade, maybe conceal the rush of confusion and embarrassment as it happened upon my face. It was happening. Relinquishing control, I found my voice deep within my gut and spoke with a tongue laced with frailty. "Karen," I managed almost inaudibly. "I have to tell you something!"

"Well, what is it?" The virginal mistress begged with languid, almond shaped eyes, the definitive image of curiosity.

"I... had sex..." Finally, it was over. The conversation had climaxed, and I could slowly regroup from the terror that is telling your best friend you are no longer an untouched flower.

"Oh! And how was that?" Shocked by my confession, Karen paused from devouring her sushi and stared relentlessly into my eyes, the very action I attempted to avoid as I hid behind a napkin dispenser.

"Uh... okay, I guess." Slowly, I regained my normal breathing routine. In and out, just like that movie starring Kevin Kline and Tom Selleck.

"Oh, okay. Who was this boy?" Karen inquired, revealing her true self, not the one I had suspected to judge me for participating in impious affairs.

"Just some guy I met on Grindr. He's cool."

"Okay. Finish your sushi, I'm gonna take you to meet my friends now." That was my very first day visiting Christopher Newport University.

Oy; that was the condensed version of my sex life. A random, no-name somebody I met on Grindr who was "cool." Not the coolest, but he sure could eat an ass. I don't have any qualms regarding the way my virginity was lost, or the nature in which we politely never spoke to one another after the incident. Brandon?[13] was **eight years** older than me, and obviously more sexually experienced than an eighteen-year-old boy who recently moved to Newport News after spending the last five years of his life in Farmville. He was twenty-six with several gray hairs forming at his temples, and delicious fingers eager to explore my body. I was impressionable. I was eager. I think I wanted to know the secret of sex so it wouldn't become this evasive entity that I'd never understand. So, when an appealing pursuer messaged me on Grindr, telling me that I was "one of the most attractive black men" he ever saw, I spotted the cock train and decided to hop on. It was the first train. I'm an easy lay. Actually, I'm a whore.

Trouble was, Grindr[14] was malfunctioning, and if working properly, he never would've viewed my profile as we were roughly two hundred miles apart.

I was still living in Farmville when Bryan? messaged me from Suffolk, Virginia. I felt an indisputable connection as he spoke of me riding him until I saw stars. Serendipitously, I formerly made plans to move in with my father for four months and I was leaving for Newport News in two days. I would go from being two hundred miles away to thirty. Something No Name, Donny? sought a much more doable distance for a virginal piece of ass whom he wanted to call him daddy. I never did. That was weird. If he was willing to pay me back child support, I'd call him daddy. Since he wanted to fuck me up the ass, I stuck with his first name. I'm not that fucked up—I don't think.[15]

---

[13] Because I fail to recall his name, I'll shift through a mental rolodex of men I *wish* I'd had sex with, followed by a question mark every time his name should come up.

[14] Grindr is a free gay dating app that alerts gay men of other gay men in the area. Generally, guys range anywhere from 100 feet to maybe even fifty miles away, unless you favorite a person, then they will forever appear on your phone, no matter how far away you happen to be.

[15] Down the road I have hooked up with guys who've made me call them

He gave me his number, and we began corresponding with each other more frequently, attempting to finalize our sexual plans. I would text him constantly until my old phone, Ricky, pulled some of his usual shit and elected to die right when I was on the verge of getting some. I lamented the universe when my cell phone screen went black and my No Name pursuer wasn't able to further explain what his intentions were for my "man pussy."

Don't fuck with a bitch with a plan. My phonebook was backed up on Google Contacts, I retrieved his number and started messaging his phone through AIM instant messaging, a form of communication equivalent to twenty-first century cave drawings. I was determined with all my might to get it in.

Two days rolled by and it was time for me to move into my father's home with Wendy before she passed, and before chapter seven was a thing. After getting my phone fixed, which took about a week, it was time for us to meet. (There was no way in hell I was going to meet a strange man without a working cell phone. Worst case scenario, if I never fixed it I could throw it at him if things went haywire and kept it moving.) We made plans for that Friday, and I did all the things my cousin and Pop suggested I do to prepare. I thoroughly cleaned my anal gland. Utilizing the anal douche I bought online a few months prior, I squirted fresh water from the shower up my rear end, and I did this until the liquid being released from inside me was crystal clear.

I asked Amethyst which outfit I should wear, and once I finished dressing and packing a few necessities (*Dentyne Ice* in my backpack), I left for James?'s pickup truck conspicuously parked at a stop sign, half a block from my house. As I approached his car, I noticed my father following me. I tried to pick up speed but my father steadily trailed closely behind, and it became fairly apparent I could not avoid an awkward encounter with the first boy who actually wanted to take me out on a date. Even if he was a graying man nearing thirty. And by *date* I mean *eat*. And by *on a date* I mean *prolly in his car*.

My father spewed general patriarchal bullshit, "Have my boy home by midnight, or he'll burst into flames. His only remains being diamonds, glitter, and dust," or I don't know. I wasn't really listening.

The ride in CJ?'s truck was different for me. I was utterly speechless for the first time in my life, and I think he could sense how unexposed I

---

daddy. I did it again and again and again. Let's just say I got over it.

was to that situation. We were at a standstill on the interstate. He took that opportunity to ease my tension. His right hand slid in between my legs, slowly raising his palm till he was firmly massaging my upper inner thigh, and began massaging my cock through my jeans. I doubt I formed two complete sentences to Chris? before we approached third base, and all I could muster from my parted lips were, "Wow... this is the best ride of my life."

We made it back to his place, a completely decent one bedroom apartment appropriate for a bachelor waiting to move up in his career field. He said he was expecting to become manager at Lowe's soon, meaning he'd be make more money, not that he needed much more. His home was perfect for him, begging the question, what is the American Dream if it is not to be upwardly mobile? I noticed that his medium sized television placed on an aging entertainment center lacked a cable box. When I asked why he didn't have one, his response was, "Oh, TV's bad for you." I knew by then when I grew up for real, not just legally, I wanted to write for television. His first strike, not counting his texting as he drove.

Looking at his extensive set of alphabetized DVDs, I saw the disgusting and alarming red flags that happened to be every *Twilight* DVD that had been released up to that point. *That* was strike two.

He asked me which movie I wanted to watch, and I chose *Just Friends* starring Anna Farris and Ryan Reynolds, because Ryan Reynolds is hot and I hadn't gotten to see his abs in that one. Sean? inserted the DVD in the player, during which time I glanced again at his DVD set and saw he owned every season of *Will & Grace*. "Bad for you" my ass, he was just cheap as hell.

Once the DVD's opening credits began, he replaced himself on the couch beside me and stared intently into my eyes. Uncomfortable for seven seconds, feeling closer to the length of a Celine Dion encore, I went for the kiss. He was the third kiss of my life. The first one was an accident in tenth grade, when a guy I thought was straight told me to sit in his lap. We played gay chicken... and well, both of us won. The second time was with a bi-curious guy I had the biggest crush on. He licked my teeth and tasted like laundry detergent. This time was much better than the second time. I couldn't tell if it was better than the first, three years had passed between them, and there's something special about your first kiss regardless.

Three minutes of making out, and we were horizontal on his couch. He was in between my legs fully clothed, thrusting his genitals against mine and exploring my tongue with his. He drew back into a sitting position as I straddled him. He tried to lift me up. He failed. I wasn't dropped, but Ivan? didn't even manage to make it off the couch, his excuse being, "I'm weak." Strike three.

I walked my ass back to his room, we made out on his bed until he left for a few seconds and came back with a towel.

"Excuse me, what's the towel for?" I asked.

He furrows a brow and smirks, "Things are gonna get messy."

I took that as I wasn't good enough to cum on his sheets. And if we're not holding anything back, to bleed either. I had never been penetrated before, and I had been told that a little bleeding is a common side effect of anal sex.

Colin? tried ripping my pants off only to realize it was a harder struggle than he originally anticipated. He asked me, "These are really tight. Are they women's jeans?"

I looked him in the eyes and said, "No, they are not." Lying like a real man.

He took my toes into his mouth, sucking on each one before he licked the sole of my foot. He lingered, I was glad for it. Daniel? flipped me over to my stomach, and slipped his tongue over my ass hole. I was in heaven, craving for him to continue as the tip of his tongue plunged its way into my body. My body screamed with appreciation, and even now, if I close my eyes, I can feel him going deeper and deeper into me, lathering my insides with the wet pressure of his mouth.

The next part I sucked at. It was penetration time. I was still on my stomach as he tried forcing his dick inside me. I felt a sharp pain pinch throughout my entire body, signaling to him it wasn't going to fit. He used fair amounts of lube. We tried several positions, he bent me over the side of the bed, we tried cowgirl, and then he gave up, deducing I could've been a top. Predictably, my little Princess WaWa had gone flaccid. Stanley? rolled off peeved, jacking himself off to prevent blue balls.

I'm not sure how I felt about anything that day. I didn't feel like a loser; I didn't feel like I was particularly into his advances, and it didn't happen. I ended up not ejaculating aside from a few stray drops of pre-cum, even after he administered fellatio. I remember thinking, "Ooh, I've gotta tell Carol about this!" when I felt his lips caressing the head of my penis.

We stopped fooling around and he napped for a bit. He woke in half an hour and cooked us a Mexican inspired tortilla dish. Strike four. You don't serve Mexican on a gay date, that's like lighting a house on fire you still plan to revisit before the smoke clears. We watched one of Tarantino's early films starring Kurt Russell and the girl from *Rent,* and I would take frequent breaks to stare at him. Night fell, and his dimly lit living room created interesting shadows contouring the curves of his face. I wanted to know the ins and outs of them all. He asked me several times why I was staring at him, my reply was his beauty. A more accurate response would've been my carnal desire.

Slowly, I went to him—it was my initiation this time. I brought my mouth to his, and once again we were horizontal, my legs stretching around his finely curved ass. We walked back to his room, this time with him making a pit stop to his bathroom to mouthwash out the taste of homemade Mexican food. I thought I was okay, hence the Dentyne Ice.

We found ourselves again in the missionary position. This time Jacob? slid his member between my ass and instead of penetrating my hole he, teased it. Within two or three minutes, I came. I liked being the aggressor. Having my first orgasmic experience with a second party, I had no idea how sex worked. Still don't.

He jacked himself off once more and then drove me home, discussing how he was really a "black woman," and why his dancing reflected more of an awkward white man despite his years watching *Living Single,* and it was a fairly pleasant ride. No lap action, though. We arrived back at my house, my father and Wendy hosting a gathering of their peers, and I kissed John? in his truck goodbye before I exited and he rode off into the distance. I went inside the house, said my hellos to everyone, then sat back in the room I shared with Amethyst and prepared to text Carol, realizing the repaired phone I received just days before was still in the car of my no name liaison.

Seventeen: Mission Jeremiah

What can I write about Karen "The Nun" Anghel that I haven't already written? She's always been there, or has been when I needed her... which was relatively often a year ago. She's a sexy Catholic girl with big boobs and no gag reflex, *and* she's still a virgin. She still believes in true love, as a twenty-one-year-old woman, odd as it may seem. I think it's noble, considering the world we live in and the one she's created for herself. Part of the reason I keep her around is her helping me believe in love and that good things can happen to good people. And I steal her chocolate and outfits when the time calls for it, but that's normal. She's the friend you call at three a.m. because you've had a few too many mixed drinks and you don't wanna call that guy you like (Derek). She's awful and funny and everything you need in your miserable, depressed life. More often, she's profoundly indifferent to the rest of the world. Based on looks alone, she could have been featured in one of those ads you see before you stream some television show illegally from your laptop. You know, the Asian girl asking if you want to play—thanks to her parents, she's not that girl. She's the one who stays in night after night in her oversized pajamas, stuffing marshmallows in her mouth, and finds the time to calm her overly gay, hypersensitive friend who requires more attention than a premature pup. And since she's one of my best friends in a very small group of people, I've never grown sick of (her, Carol, and Pop, etc.). I'll try to make this quick so it doesn't end up a twenty page love letter about friendship, growing, and all that other nonsense. I'm too good a writer to succumb to that bullshit.

We met, unremarkably, on the drama team. She was Ms. Fast's bitch. Her official title was Sound Girl, mainly serving as the auteur's personal assistant. We made nice. She was easy to speak to.

We didn't become Thelma and Louise until tenth grade, when she and I had driver's ed together. I'd been spending more and more time with her and Carol, and driver's ed was like our alone time. Granted that included the more fabulous queen of fashion, Ginnifer Thompson, and the well-spoken sarcastic Republican, Johnny Gribble.

Our class coincided with tenth grade gym, so there were many days when Coach Scott would leave us outside by the track to go tend to his more pressing ventures. Coach's billable hours were spent viewing a basketball game, or checking on his ice cream truck that he'd drive around campus, soliciting children with endless amounts of sugar, if they had the money—aiding and abetting institutionalized obesity through Nutty Buddy trafficking, the new crack. He's everyone's favorite gym teacher. Fact.

It was one of those days by the track, we were all sitting around with nothing particular required of us that day, other than texting someone else who was actually doing shit with their lives. Without any motivating factors, I prepared to take a walk around the track until I grew tired or it was time to report to a class which had a much more obvious objective. Like, maybe even on a chalkboard or something.

Taking notice of the day, it was nice enough weather that if I kept an even pace and if the breeze retained its continuous speed, I could make it completely around the circumference a couple times without accumulating too much sweat. I had my Ricky with quite the library of illegally downloaded tunes, and a random spur of optimism. I was totally gonna go crush that shit. When I announced to my usual clique I would be taking a lap or two, Karen, as only she can be, was eager to volunteer to join me. My solo stride grew into a two person event, and I wasn't complaining.

Lightly conversing about the never-ending strife and drama which is adolescent life, the graduating seniors and the drama club passed through our mouths a time or two, leading us to purposefully land on the topic of one Jeremiah Jobs, the lanky, blue-eyed, lovable jackass playing the lead that year in the ill-fated *Property Rites*. He was at least six foot two and covered with acne—his face, anyway. Perhaps there was a charm to his outrageous lunacy that pervaded Karen's private thoughts, and I somehow remained aloof to his supposed enchantment. Therefore, I was shocked when Karen admitted she had a crush on him. Like, I lost my shit. Literally. I wear diapers now.

In the midst of one of her infamous never-ending run-ons, "...and I can't believe I'm telling you this, but when Dillip[16] asked me out I didn't know what to do because I had talked to Carol and Katherine (Karen's

---

[16] Dillip, Jeremiah's best friend and drama team alum who asked out Karen knowing she and Jeremiah had some feelings for one another.

sister, two years younger, born on the same day) and decided I was going to ask Jeremiah out to the movies the day before Dill asked me, which was weird because they're best friends. Anyways, I said yes to Dill even though I heard that Jeremiah liked me."

"Look at you, Karen, driving a wedge between a friendship of gargantuan proportions." They weren't Rosencrantz and Guildenstern, but let's just say I started a rumor that the two thespians were shagging backstage. I was impressed that since knowing her, this was the first time Karen took interest in a real live boy you could see, touch and feel. Not that empiricism's all it's cracked up to be.

"Yeah, and I actually tried to fill out one of those things on Facebook or Myspace where it's like a survey and you're answering questions about how you feel about certain things, and somehow it was relevant to Jeremiah, and I ended up typing this really long block of things that turned into a seven or eight page confession that I have saved on my computer." She spoke nervously. I could see in her eyes that something inside her was forcing her to tell me. She wanted to fight it but couldn't.

"Holy shit! Karen, you have to give it to him!" I'm that friend. I give great advice.

"I mean, I don't know. He's going to graduate in like a month and it's really long, and I don't even know if it's good writing." She had a whole host of reasons why her confession would disrupt the Earth's rotation, striking epic disaster. I smelled bullshit. Not literally, my diaper's still dry...

ANYWAY... "You have to! Think about it, what do you have to lose? He's going away in a month, it isn't like he can also confess his love for you too, it'll just be this thing you get off your chest before you forever part." I'm thoroughly grossed out by my former self.

"I don't know. It's really long. I mean, it's seven pages, and you're the only one I told."

I was surprised. "Not Carol, not Katherine?"

"No, I haven't told either of them, I don't think. Maybe I mentioned something to Katherine but even she doesn't even have the full story I don't think, and I don't know."

Believing I possessed an intuition privileged only to myself, Oprah, and God in that order, I continued, "Karen, you told me. You didn't tell Katherine, or Carol, you told your loudmouth best friend, and you knew as the words were coming out of your mouth what I was going to tell you to do. I think you want to give it to him or otherwise you would've told Katherine or Carol."

Whimpering like a five-year-old who was told recess is over, she said, "But I don't know, it's weird. I can't give it to him, it's too weird."

Time to put up your blocks, bitch! "Uh... if you print it out, I could hand it to him."

Scrunching up her nose awkwardly, the angelic frame of her face tensed to the right and relaxed to the left, as it often did while weighing life-changing decisions. "I don't know... are you sure?"

"Yes, I'm more than sure! Karen, you told *ME*! I think you even know for yourself this is what you want to do, but you need me to bring it out of you. That's the only reason you'd confide something of such magnitude, and you know it! Besides, all you're doing is telling him how you feel before he leaves your life forever. No big deal."

"I guess you're right. God, the shit you talk me into!"

"You wouldn't have told me if you didn't wanna be talked into it." By then it was our third or fourth time taking a lapping the track, meaning it was time for us to go soon, given we move at a solid nonagenarian pace. How does Betty White shuffle so quickly?

The next day slugged by as third block approached. Our driver's ed class was to watch a basketball game in the school gym. Karen looked at me all business, opened her black eight-inch binder, and handed over seven pages of pure soul which she neatly folded into thirds, stuffed into a plain white envelope, and handed over to me. I began scribing a message alluding to the power hidden within such a non-confrontational envelope, and Karen promptly put an end to the Shakespearean sonnet I was forging on the front.

"No, it's going to be blank when you hand it to him." Within seconds she whipped another blank envelope out of her binder, opened the last one, carefully relocated the contents to the new one, and sealed it tight. During the process I noticed she had three or four extra envelopes. When I asked her why, she replied, "Because you're you and I know you could be Waldell and write a Shakespearean sonnet on the cover of one. I need back up with you." Fair enough.

I took out my agenda book and had Coach Scott sign it, listing the bathroom as my intended destination. He complied with unusually minimum interrogation and I was off to see The Wizard, or Mr. Jackson. Walking into his class, Jackson greeted me as he normally did with a huge smile and an open door. I love that man. Looking around the room several times, I noticed Jeremiah was absent, and out of desperation to ensure he'd receive the letter today, I left the letter in the hands of Jackson with the instruction to give it to Jeremiah when he returned from whatever the hell he was doing. Presumably, regular dopy Farmvillian things. Like sneaking off to get a large sweet tea—always a big deal.

I made it back to the gym and perched myself next to Karen. She asked how it went. I said that I wouldn't know because he wasn't in the room and I left it in the hands of Jackson. She nodded, "Okay." And that was the last we spoke of Mission Jeremiah that day. I texted her after we went to our respective homes, making sure her brains were still intact and she didn't regret the happenings earlier. She answered no and that whatever happened, happened. No big deal. I could sense as the once prominent serial texter friend of Karen, the slightest hint of a subtle lie.

Inevitably she had to tell Carol and Katherine, and they both read all seven pages after I forced Karen's hand in delivering the message to Jeremiah. I wonder if Hermes was as invested in the outcome of his messages as I was with Karen and Jeremiah's. The next day Jeremiah stated he returned some of the same feelings, and he and Karen should talk soon—only they were both so damn shy. They would be in a room together and not look at one another, coyly ignoring the other's presence; it made me sick. Two days later I walked into Fast's classroom first block, and there stood Jeremiah to the left and Karen to the right, speaking to their respective social groups. And then I made my arrival known:

"HEY KAREN! HEY JEREMIAH! HOW ARE YOU TWO?" As Tina Fey once said, "Bitches get shit done."

"Uh… fine, I guess?" Karen replied, swallowing the bitter taste of my friendship before eight in the morning.

"Yeah, we're cool." Jeremiah noted.

"That's great! You guys should talk about important stuff, because that's really worth talking about, you know. Important things." Their eyes drifted over to me.

Karen exploded, "You fucking bitch! I hate you! Why am I your friend? I hope you fucking die!" Although her mouth didn't move once. She said it with her eyes.

They both fell silent, leaving me to skip out of homeroom jovially; I got my point across. It didn't have the effect I wanted, the nothing they said in the room with me was the most they'd spoken to each other directly for years.

He was graduating soon so they signed each other's yearbooks. Hers received a sloppily scrawled paragraph promising they had more to speak about and that he felt they were going to see one another "a lot this summer." I read it and giggled because I'm a nimrod. Katherine read it and giggled because Karen's her sister. When Karen would read and reread it, she'd turn bright red because it was actually happening to her, and when Carol read it she was skeptical. Carol didn't think grand gestures were the way to go about telling someone you like them. She hates romantic comedies and explicit joy. There was definitely a lesbian lurking around in there somewhere.

Jeremiah graduated, he and Karen continued to correspond via text message. Over the course of the summer, days turned into weeks and there were no signs of Jeremiah attempting to see Karen, and most of us bet that he was saving his grand gestures for Karen's eighteenth birthday party to be held at her house in mid-June. Everyone had an invitation, and you just didn't say no to an Anghel party. Everyone with a computer on Katherine and Karen's friends list were welcome. Karen made sure she texted Jeremiah distinctly to ensure his attendance. He texted her back midday saying he'd think about it.

Naïve as I am, I believed he would show up. I thought he was for Karen and wanted her to be happy. I'd offer lavish fairy tales of Jeremiah riding through at the last minute because he was caught in traffic on the interstate and had to take a detour, having to drive his grandma to the hospital while waiting for an elephant to cross the road as it gave birth. Then upon birth, the infant calf wouldn't have been able to breathe so Jeremiah'd have to save its life with one hand while giving his grandmother chest compressions with the other, resurrecting Dumbo and making an oxygen tank out of gum wrappers, rubber bands, the elephant's placenta and a nearby plant for his grandmother. Jeremiah would then strap a thousand birds to the roof and the back of his car so it could fly, instead of driving which would mean he'd have to wait in traffic. He'd give his grandmother a parachute and push her out of the airborne automobile as they flew past the hospital in order to direct the birds to Karen's with just enough time left to swoop in and kiss Karen beneath the stars and full moon as we all cheered. Her mother would cry, her father would look for his gun and her brother would pretend like nothing was happening.

Nothing happened. Karen ended the night sitting on her back porch talking to a hot guy. Although, grievously for Karen, it was me. Night came, candles were blown out, the cake was cut, cars were leaving, remaining guests were yawning and there were no birds swirling in the sky, lowering a car unto the Earth, releasing the night's main event. He never showed up. No more ifs, maybes, possiblys, could haves, might haves, and certainly no more hope. The one thing I gave her was gone, now.

I looked at her, the crickets singing in the background as the cool summer breeze blew past us. I didn't want to ask her how she felt, I didn't have to.

"He texted me earlier today; I thought he was going to make it. But, I guess not." Her voice was quiet, like it gets before she tires of exhaustion—there was a sadness in the belly of her words now.

"What did he say when you texted him?" I leaned back on my elbows as Karen hunched over fiddling with her toes. I spent the time conversing, partially searching for the Big Dipper, and Karen, aside from periodically breaking to text someone back, remained focused on her feet.

"He said he'd think about it. I thought he was going to come because he wrote in my yearbook that we were going to see each other a lot over the summer, and we haven't seen each other once. And you kept saying, he's going to come and kiss you under the stars and all that stuff. I guess not." Her brother came out with one of the friends he'd made on his soccer team, keeping relative distance as they shot Nerf guns off in the red mud and patchy backyard. The background whining ceased. He scared the crickets.

I pulled up and forced myself to face Karen, all seriousness. I looked into her eyes and told her, "You know, I really wanted this for you."

She looked back at me, narrowly missing a Styrofoam bullet and said, "Yeah, me too." Not too long after that, Johanson arrived to drive me and Carol home, and at Karen's next party on the Fourth of July we discovered Jeremiah had acquired a girlfriend. And that bastard broke my heart. The worst part still, is that he broke Karen's.

Eighteen: The Gay? Luck Club

A strange thing happens to a guy when he realizes all his close friends from high school are a little gay, and they didn't all start out that way. Since graduating from Prince Edward County High School, Cann came out as bisexual, moved to northern Massachusetts and is dating a girl named Marjorie. My best friend Karen came out as pansexual; she's dating a female-to-male transman who lives in Canada. A week ago, my best friend Johnny came out as bi (which I'm sure will turn into gay in three months), and I told him to download Grindr. Now he has a boyfriend. And me, I have Netflix and Nutella. Just ain't right.

Actually I lied; I can't really afford Nutella, and my father's house is devoid of WiFi. Even the pathetic fake life I give myself is more glamorous than reality. How many different ways can I put it? I'm alone. Enough with the digressions, though, I'm sure they're to be expected by now.

This is all very shocking because for four years, I was the only gay guy. Scratch that, I was *the* gay guy. Sure there were other homos, other obviously-gay-waiting-till-college lgbtqqiaaspuudfmkknwyxx members dying to come sashaying out of the closet in their Jimmy Choo knock-offs, belting some dated Cher ballad while blowing the nearest meat stick within reach, but they knew better than to hold any exclusive press releases in the cafeteria or experiment with non-gender conforming apparel while in high school. The fun stuff had to wait until university.

With this knowledge, I could say the one I predicted was Cann. I knew Karen was different and I've always felt like there are things she's hiding from me, not revealing the full truth about herself or her past. She will always be a mystery to me, that's part of her allure. Then there's Johnny. The boy who mentioned in tenth grade he participated in sexual intercourse with a man he met online, and liked it! Thereafter, he said it was a fluke and that it'd probably never happen again. Two and a half years post-graduation—four years later, I am informed via Facebook instant messaging that he is a power bottom who doesn't mind the company of black men. I wasn't expecting that from my Caucasian Republican comrade who had a religious breakthrough senior year and found Jesus. Now he found black dick.[17] Oh how times have changed.

I think of these three people often because I love them dearly. Their influence has incredibly affected my life in high school and how I view myself now. My joy is attributed to them and it's wonderful that now they're meeting their true selves. First, I saw the differences they were making in fashion. Karen began wearing skinny jeans; Cann fancied her flannel (That's not a tasteless lesbian joke, I swear. It's coincidentally true), and Johnny... Johnny kinda started giving a shit. It was invigorating to see the people I've loved transform into individuals they now felt comfortable to love too. Even more exciting, one can note, is I can take more than my share of credit for their revelations in how they've expressed themselves across the lgbtqqiaaspskljdvbehrbflaskdjcnsmcjjjjjj spectrum. Would they be who they are now if I wasn't myself so consistently boisterous and gaudy? I don't think so... I'm lying, but something has to go in this chapter.

I can vividly recall on the first day of school I opted to wear a shirt from the women's section in Sears. I just went shopping with my good friend, Reba Lee. After saving up around three hundred sixty dollars of lunch money and birthday gifts that I reserved and placed securely under my bed, I convinced my mom to take me and Reba Lee to the mall. We went crazy dropping cash everywhere we could find a decent discount; right before we left, Reba Lee and her friend Collisha helped me make the bravest decision of my life—to be myself when I went back to school on Monday.

Prince Edward was hardly a site of unprejudiced acceptance. People would call me names that eventually flew by me like a blur. I resolved long ago for those occurrences in which I was berated, I should live in my own fantasy world. A world where I was a fashion model and they were Sarah Jessica Parker taking notes for next fall.

There I was, Naomi Campbelling it down the hallway, working every angle before I made it to my first block class, ready for anything. That morning before school, I stared in my bathroom mirror for thirty minutes, telling myself to expect the worst from school peers. "They're going to hate it. No one else will get it. You be you. They'll laugh at you,

---

[17] One can love Jesus and black dick simultaneously and unironically.

make fun of you, but that is okay. You're not doing it for them. You're doing it for yourself." I didn't have any mentor or wise older gender bending queen to follow. Pop came later. For reasoning beyond myself, I determined since I didn't have a friend who could provide me the support I needed, I was going to be that friend to myself. I made it to first block without being murdered by homophobic schoolmates. So far, so good.

Mrs. Lupas's classroom was nearly empty as to be expected at half past seven, I walked to the second row of desks, placed my vomit-green, black marker fucked book bag on the floor, and turned around bending to sit when it happened.

Ginny, the more attractive version of Sarah Jessica Parker, sat down across from me with her athletic then boyfriend, Demarkus. I heard her say, "Hello Waldell!" before giving my outfit a once over. Then she... laughed hysterically. There is no other way to put it. Sheer, unrestrained laughter vibrated throughout her entire body, erupting from the hottest girl in tenth grade. There's no other sentiment that forms an accurate description; it wasn't out of spite or hatred or judgment. I was wearing a medium women's T-shirt with butterflies made out of blue rhinestones, fitted jeans and my newly purchased black and white sneakers that completely downgraded the ensemble—I was learning after all—and she continued outlandishly snickering.

Ginny and I were friends. I knew I caught her off guard. She apologized, not needing to. And that, thankfully, was the absolute worst of it. Indubitably, people talked and said things in the hallways—nothing ever really came of their gossip. I was indeed wearing a woman's shirt. I was shopping in the women's section. And by day two, they were pretty much over it.

In all my newfound glory, I began improving myself, as one does. I learned there were luscious benefits in taking risks with fashion; I even started wearing makeup. What started as eyeliner gradually became eyeshadow, and then mascara. I began adding wings at the corners of my eyelids. They eventually became as much a staple as my wearing shoes on my feet. Speaking of which, I figured I could squeeze my fat-ass toes into a woman's size eleven and a half wide, if I tried hard enough. Once, I ordered boots online from Target that came straight to my mother's house. My stepfather got the mail and told my mother what

I purchased. She investigated whether or not they were women's boots. I had to think of a lie quickly before she rebuked my privilege to wear them.

"Yes ma, I got them from the men's section."

"Then why does it say 'wmn' on the side of the box?" she protested. Like she *always* did.

"It's an acronym. It stands for: Western Men's Network!" Denial is a beautiful thing; she bought it.

I lied to my mother a lot that year. I would do my makeup after she left the house, and before I went home after school I'd have a change of clothes with me. If I rode home with someone, which would happen often because of drama practice or hanging with Reba Lee, I could change my total monstrosity within the blink of an eye. The driver wouldn't even know what hit them, as if they turned away for a second and saw Cinderella immediately after the clock struck twelve. Hectic as it was, that was a large part of my life from tenth grade until graduation.

It was this past summer when my mother finally caught on to the fact that I wear makeup. I was leaving the house to revisit Reba Lee, and she spotted me. It cracks me up to remember how appalled she looked when I told her I'd been applying makeup since I was fifteen. She saw me done up weeks after my nineteenth birthday.

Being that fabulous isn't all perks. I had a tough time with teachers who thought I should dress more masculine. My Spanish teacher, one of my closest confidants who even bought Ricky Martin's memoir for me, suggested, "See, you should be more like him." He is a pretty handsome savant.

"But I'm not like Ricky Martin, Mrs. Lupas. I'm like myself. This is how I like to dress. I'm seventeen years old. Let me find my way!" We had that argument biweekly, I'd say. She'd typically be the person who drove me home from school if drama practice wasn't in session, and when we weren't discussing Picasso or Kahlo, or even the truth-telling ability of Shakira's hips, we'd always review why I felt the need to don such outrageous apparel. Thinking now, I would say because the world is my stage, but that sounds too damn gay.

And there's more to lose than your Spanish teacher's approval. Recently, I've accepted that I don't think there could ever be someone to love me. When you are a character, when you're larger than life or are a polarizing person, not everyone is going to react to you the same way. Everyone has obtuse emotions toward you, and it's cumbersome for some people to relate to you or understand you because you don't fit in one of their boxes. People operate with clearly marked labels: black or white, gay or straight, feminine or masculine, and when someone cannot adhere to the restraints of strict binaries, they are often disregarded or devalued, thanks to a limiting system that does not value the many various facets of humanity. I am both feminine and masculine, am both gay and straight, and surprisingly enough, black and white. I know deep down I will never be in love or be loved back because my box is a little wider than most. It's larger than most. It's louder than most. There will probably never be a man in my life because of this. I'd rather have a large-ass lopsided box than conform to someone else's. I'm too fucking special, so I'll be alone and love myself more instead.

For a time, I didn't think that was necessarily true, but reactions from Grindr and OkCupid users enlightened me. I either have to be a drag queen, transsexual, or woman for my identity to make sense to some people. I am a cisgender male who occasionally wears makeup and might dress in drag three or four times a year. I am not a drag queen because I am not in possession of *that* fierceness. I am not a transsexual because I was assigned male at birth and I identify as male. I am not a woman because I am not a woman. Some women do have penises and they are still women. My penis is a man's because I am a man. Can I make this any clearer? I urinate standing up.

It isn't uncommon for the world to reject me; I turn to my people when I have no one else. Karen Anghel, Cann Johanson, and Johnny Gribble. We were all in high school together; we all suffered together and we're all surviving, in one way or the other, together. It may have taken them a while longer to uncover and explore facts about themselves—they never had to witness Ginny losing her shit before the first period bell rang—but slowly, they are all creating their own boxes. It's extraordinary to witness your friends becoming even better people, even braver souls than they were before. Yes, it's scary and sometimes you'll want to step in and shield their eyes from the ugliness of the world and the restless hatred that's poisoned humanity, but it's their journey. And they're never going to actually be themselves if you're always stepping in as some weird-ass gay Mother Goose protecting her flamboyant eggs. If they crack, they crack. Just be there to put the pieces back together if they do. I just listen when they suffer... keeping quiet is hard for me since I've been living my life out loud for so long. It's their time, their stories. I've had my moment in the spotlight and have luxuriated under the indulgent glow. No more Naomi Campbelling it down the hallway, it's their turn to strut. And I know I've had very little to do with their stories. They've had their own crosses to bear and it's foolish of me to take credit for something as personal as coming out, BUT DEAR GOD... no one loves me. I have no Netflix, no Nutella, no WiFi and no Ben & Jerry's. Please God, let me have this!

Nineteen: Colorblind

Derek Island never loved me. Not at all, not even a little bit. I can admit it now. It doesn't hurt nearly as much anymore. I couldn't tell how many times I've lain awake at night debating whether or not he actually cared for me, or was simply pleased by the idea of me. I know it sounds cliché, but if good ol' Dare always kept me in his clutches he'd never have to end up alone. He made a very big mistake, and I let him. He made me think I was lovable. I know people care about me. I have Cann and Karen, my sisters. my mother and Jesus, but Derek made me feel like someone could really want to be with me. That he'd want to wake up and find me next to him in bed or go to sleep with our arms wrapped around each other every night. This was all a lie, and I allowed myself to believe it. It was what I wanted. I wanted to be wrong about why I hated Ryan Murphy. I wanted the bells and whistles, the long kisses and endless nights, and the limitless conversations that would last decades. I wanted the house, the husband, and babies. And I wanted Derek. No one ever believed in me like he did. No one read my work or encouraged me to keep going. No one cared to. I've never been quite that important to anyone.

And admitting this carved out chunks of my heart. I forgot how to be self-sufficient or loving. When Derek left for Kentucky, he robbed me of every kind thought or well wish I could ever think to hope for him. And it hurt. Part of it still hurts. Not because Derek doesn't want me, but because of what he took from me. I'd never been in love like that before, nor had I ever wanted to be, and I was crushed. There was an innocence there that I'll never retrieve—I gave it to him when I wasn't even paying attention, and he didn't even want it in the first place. One asinine mistake, and the only endless nights I knew were the nights I'd toss and turn in bed agonizing over why he didn't feel anything. I didn't know the severity of my condition until Karen talked to me about it one night, and told me how I've changed since he left, and the sadness that overtook me. Our story, the one of Derek and I, ends bitterly. I always knew it would.

I was perusing in a shoe store close in Farmville, when he messaged me:

August 17, 2013, 3:15 PM

Dare Island: *Lol. It's my first relatively free time to talk to you.*
Me: *I figured that. How's the job and your new soulmate? Lol*
Dare Island: *It's interesting. I'm working on fitting in with the organization. Made friends immediately. I like everyone and one guy a little too much. Basic Derek.*
Me: *Yeah, I figured. Exciting though, right? Do you or don't you just love Kentucky?*
Dare Island: *I guess. I do not love it. I like it. I accept it. I am open to it. I have made out with him twice and I been here a week. I'm retarded.*
Me: *You're just gay. Trust me, only making out with him makes you kinda like the Virgin Mary according to gay standards.*
Dare Island: *I like him. But I need to chill. I'm such an intense person. I need to take a step back.*
Me: *I don't know if that's okay. If you really want him, I say go for him. Life is too short to be overly cautious with your heart. He could be your Big.*
Dare Island: *If there's one thing all past relationships have taught me, I am someone's Big. For once I would like someone to seek my shoulder. To lay in my lap. Which he does... but I hate the girly emotions. I want someone to see their rock when they look at me.*
Me: *Dare, that doesn't happen immediately. It takes time, normally months, for more severe cases maybe even years. You just have to decide if it's worth the wait. And if it's not, you're gonna have to enjoy the single life until you find someone worth waiting for.*
Dare Island: *Meh. I'm your rock. On occasion.*
Me: *That took half a decade. Is this man worth it, or is he worth finding out if it is?*
Dare Island: *Everyone is worth it. I wouldn't trade you for anything at this point.*

I'm pretty sure that point has long since passed.

Me: *And I wouldn't trade you, and this may sound incredibly cynical of me, but not everyone is worth it, at least not to everybody.*

Dare Island: *It's okay to think that. Wrong, but okay :)*

Me: *Okay, but sometimes you put in the work and people are not who you thought they were. That's the chance you take when you dare to love someone.*

Dare Island: *But the experience they left you with is everything. There are memories I would die to keep. Read* Annabelle Lee.

Me: *Everything is not* Annabelle Lee. *Sometimes life is Precious, the morbidly obese raped kind.*

Dare Island: *You don't remember* Precious *for how sad. You remember how she kept going and kept going. Get it together cynic.*

Me: *You remember the pain she went through, the never ending struggle of her life, and you ask yourself, is it worth it? Was it worth it? Maybe I just feel too much. Lol*

Dare Island: *Maybe you're a wimp.*

Me: *And how would that make me a wimp Mr. Streep?*

Dare Island: *You're moving from wimp territory into cunt.*

Last time I'll ever refer to him as the greatest actor of all time.

Me: *Well, given your diverse sexual history, I imagine that shouldn't be much of a challenge for you.*

Later that evening, I forwarded messages between Karen and me to Derek.

Me: *Dare's met someone else, and if he marries this kid you're fucking coming to the wedding with me.*

Karen: *I will gladly keep your flask in my purse during the ceremony and hold your hand through the copious amounts of alcohol you'll be consuming at the reception and make sure you don't make some awful speech whilst inebriated.*

The very next day, Dare appeared to have had a drink or two himself.

August 18, 2013, 1:25 PM

Dare Island: *I miss you.*
Me: *What do you mean?*
Dare Island: *Just having issues lol*
Me: (referring to the night before when he mentioned he'd been drinking) *Clearly; still drunk?*
Dare Island: *No.*
Me: *It's a good thing you miss me, it appears the effect I have on all my guys.*
Dare Island: *All your guys? Lol*
Me: *Stories for some other time, love. :)* Time, meaning in two minutes.
Dare Island: *Lol ok.*
Me: *A couple guys I hooked up with are eager for me to return to CNU is all.* I can only recall one. Pretty sure I was lying in terms of plurality.
Dare Island: *Ohhhhhhh. Your love for me is waning.*
Me: *Kyle is his name. He's sweet, uncircumcised and cums like a fire hose. Only a couple inches taller than me. Wanna see?*
Dare Island: *Uhhhhh. Nah. Lol*
Me: *But he's so cute with his beard. It tickles!*
Dare Island: *Omg. I'm happy for you.*
Me: *I'm not sure if there's much to be happy for. I liked sucking him off and he'd eat me out. He was fun. He always pressured me to cuddle, maybe I'll give that a shot now. Maybe I'm ready to give this relationship thing a shot... Thoughts?*
Dare Island: *Shoot for the moon.*
Me: *Isn't this great? I'm finally expressing my sexuality. There's Tim, the only black guy I ever dated, but he's hardcore romantic and knows where my spot is, that could be dangerous. I like Bryan?, but I could never date him. He despises network television.*
Dare Island: *What is your purpose in all this? If I was pouting about Justin you'd get all pissy.*
Me: *I don't think I did the last time? Or did I?*
Dare Island: *I sent one text. You're being a Dick.*
Me: *How so, sir?*
Dare Island: *Trying to make me jealous.*

Me: *I'd be lying if I said I wasn't, so I'm sorry. But you can talk to me about your liaisons; I will be okay if I hear about them from time to time.*

August 20, 2013, 7:45 AM

Me: *John Travolta and Miley Cyrus – I Thought I Lost You.*

August 21, 2013, 11:04 PM

Dare Island: *Marry me.*
Me: *All you had to do was ask...*

August 22, 2013, 8:36 AM

Dare Island: *Lol*
Me: *You couldn't handle being married to me.*
Dare Island: *Prob not lol*
Me: *But imagine how much fun we'd have in our short lived matrimony.*
Dare Island: *Barely any.*
Me: *What makes you say that?*
Dare Island: *I'd kill you.*
Me: *But the making up would be insane. You'd either be my Richard Burton or my Hubbell Gardiner.*
Dare Island: *'Cause you'd word your apology as an acceptance of one I didn't give and I'd choke you out.*
Me: *Not to mention I'm thinner and younger than you. I can't wait; it sounds like so much fun! ;D*
Dare Island: *I'd crush you.*
Me: *Is that when we'd make love?*
Dare Island: *No. When we would fuck. Making love is not a thing.*
Me: *It totally is, or we could make it one.*

Dare Island: *I have never 'made love' I have had sex, fucked, slept with...*

Me: *You need to make love. How many of those people were you truly in love with?*

Dare Island: *Not one. I guess that's sad.*

Me: *It is. Nigga, we need to make love.*

Dare Island: *One. Do not ever call me a Nigga and two. We will not be making love.*

I should've taken his word on the latter assertion.

Me: *Haha, it worked in Boondocks. :(Why no love making?*

August 25, 2013, 7:19 PM

Dare Island: *You got your wish. He friendzoned me lol*

It was around these days I started feeling like shit. Chapter fifteen was born my first day I returned to university...

September 1, 2013, 7:42 PM

Me: *I love you.*
Dare Island: *I love you, too.*

September 2, 2013, 12:34 AM

Dare Island: *Join the peace core with me.*
Me: *I would, but I'm a deplorable human being.*
Dare Island: *Me too. Maybe it will help us.*
Me: *It may just give me gas.*

September 5, 2013, 5:05 AM

Me: *I actually love you a lot, and it's really stupid not talking to you even though I feel like that's what I needed for a little bit. Miss you, hope all is well.*

September 8, 2013, 1:35 PM

Me: *I miss you.*
Dare Island: *Do you?*
Me: *I do. Every day.*
Dare Island: *How?*
Me: *What do you mean, how?*
Dare Island: *How do you miss me. In your writing? In your mind?*
Me: *I'm lying in bed and I wish you were here next to me. I talk to guys everyday who want to fuck and leave me, but I wanna save all my kisses for you. I wanna stare into your eyes for long periods of time and feel your arms around me as I listen to the rhythm of your heartbeat. I miss being next to you. I miss you being inside my brain; I miss you being inside my body. I miss you making my day better and making me feel less crazy. I miss dreams about you and the possibility of what we could've become. I miss your arms, your legs, your eyes, the sound of your voice, the way your words wrapped around my heart. I miss the way you smelled and miss the way you made me feel. I miss you mostly in the ways I've never had you.*
Dare Island: *You always checkmate me in the poetry department.*
Me: *Now you know you are missed!*
Dare Island: *I miss you too.*
Me: *How so?*
Dare Island: *I miss the devotion. Your public declarations to me. My private ones to you. I miss you telling me everyday how you want to be with me and then acting like you didn't the next day. I miss your wit. The singularity and individuality of your opinions. I miss that awkward three note laugh when you'd hear my flirting. I miss looking at you with your feet up with a glass of wine keeping me company while I cook you dinner. I miss the way you don't care how I'm slightly overweight. I miss all the things I never said I'd miss.*

Me: *I think we just composed a country song.*
Dare Island: *Kid Rock and Sheryl Crow.*

September 10, 2013, 12:47 PM

Me: *Dare, when we hung out this summer, why didn't you kiss me?*

September 11, 2013, 8:37 AM

Dare Island: *I didn't want to.*
Me: *Okay! Starting this morning off on a high note.*
Dare Island: *It's not a personal thing. It's just that life isn't quite as magical and pretty as it is depicted.*
Me: *It's fine. Dare, I was just curious! How're you?*
Dare Island: *Good.*
Me: *That's great.*

I was dying inside. I stopped hanging out in Karen's dorm like I normally would on the weekends. As I prayed for, I don't think anyone noticed, so they didn't ask very many questions when we'd bump into one another on campus.

September 12, 2013, 3:58 AM

I couldn't sleep. I texted myself.

ME: *I don't think he ever really had the desire to be with me. I think he appreciated me and respected who I was, underlying my wistful fantasies grew the suspicion of something I already knew: he never wanted me. He never had passion for who I was, never craved and longed for my body or for me to be in his bed. He liked the idea of stability I afforded him, as the fall back crush, or relationship alternative when other life courses failed. No, he never wanted me. He was always a great friend to me and cultivated the essence of my spirit through kindness, encouragement, and understanding. And that was enough. I've found, at 3:56 AM, Thursday, September 12, 2013, that I can move on from Derek Island and all the false hope I'd given myself this past year. Now, I'm just going to be myself.*

It sounded pretty to me at the time. I wish it really worked like that.

October 13, 2013, 2:41 PM

Me: *Any boys on the radar? And listen to Sirens by Cher.*

Her new album came out, I was addicted to the last four tracks on the disk.

Dare Island: *No, of course not.*
Me: *And why not, stud?*
Dare Island: *Don't call me that. And no one sees me as sexy.*
Me: *Okay. Have you seen* The Michael J Fox Show *or* The Crazy Ones?
Dare Island: *No*
Me: *They're fabulous! I love them. David E Kelley who created* Ally McBeal, *my favorite series of all time, created* The Crazy Ones *starring Robin Williams and Sarah Michelle Gellar as an off-beat father-daughter relationship. Kelly Clarkson guest starred on the first episode and sang alongside the dreamy James Wolk. It's really worth a watch. I promise.*
Dare Island: *How on earth did you move to this topic?*
Me: *I'm hooked on crack now.*
Dare Island: *No kidding?*
Me: *Actually, I needed to steer the conversation from you feeling bad about yourself. I feel like you only talk to me when you feel bad about yourself.*
Dare Island: *Ummmmm... You asked. I answered. My mistake.*
Me: *No harm, no foul, my good sir.*
Dare Island: *You misread that. I'm pissed at you. Which I'm not sure I've ever been before... What fun... New territory.*
Me: *Good. Be pissed. I'm so afraid.*

Dare Island: *What the fuck is your problem?*
Me: *I'm not too sure you deserve to know.*
Dare Island: *Do you forget I asked how YOU were first? That would've been a significant moment to reveal whatever malfunction is glitching your normally beautiful self???*
Me: *I don't think I want to.*
Dare Island: *I wish you would.*

Roughly two hours later

Me: *I hope you're happy.*
Dare Island: *Talk to me.*
Me: *Okay. I miss you. I'm behaving badly.*
Dare Island: *Why?*
Me: *Why what? I don't know if you knew this or not, but you're one of my favorite scars.*

Another reference to my Cher *Closer to the Truth* addiction.

Dare Island: *I'm flattered.*
Me: *The thing about scars is, they're still scars, and they wound sometimes.*[18]

October 20, 2013, 4:47 AM

Me: *Are you still mad at me?*
Dare Island: *No.*
Me: *Good. How're you?*
Dare Island: *Good. You?*
Me: *Great! Fall break, catching up on my shows!*
Dare Island: *Good!*
Me: *And you?*

---

[18] A horribly mixed reference with *Favorite Scars* and *If I Could Turn Back Time.*

Dare Island: *Watching* V for Vendetta.
Me: *Sounds like you.*
Dare Island: *Yup.*
Me: *Enjoying yourself?*
Dare Island: *Yeah, tired.*
Me: *That's good, right? You love being on your feet.*
Dare Island: *Yeah. Just makes for lacking conversation. Lol*
Me: *The important thing is, you're enjoying what you do.*
Dare Island: *I do. Now what's wrong with you?*
Me: *What do you mean?*
Dare Island: *From before.*
Me: *PMS?*
Dare Island: *Nice try.*
Me: *You never know.*
Dare Island: *So...*
Me: *So...*
Dare Island: *I'm waiting...*
Me: *For...?*
Dare Island: *An explanation.*
Me: *I was having a bad day.*
Dare Island: *Ok lol*
Me: *See, nothing too bad.*

October 23, 2013, 3:37 PM

Me: *Are you happy?*
Dare Island: *Yes.*
Me: *I'm glad!*
Dare Island: *Are you?*
Me: *I'm trying.*

October 26, 2013, 6:28 PM

Me: *I miss being your friend.*
Dare Island: *Tired of being in love with me?*
Me: *It only made the world gray and every song sad.*

Dare Island: *For all your preaching of how magical it is.*

Me: *That's funny, because I never did, but you always claimed I did.*

Dare Island: *Either way, you over it now?*

Me: *No.*

Dare Island: *Why not?*

Me: *I keep hoping one day you'll wake up and want me, but that's not going to happen and I figured I would stop or be used to it by now, but it still sucks. And ironically, I miss being your friend and having you to tell these things to. Meanwhile, I'm sorry for unloading. I hope you have an excellent weekend.*

Dare Island: *I'm sorry. I'm in a show ;) I'll text you after. I wouldn't say never.*

Two and a half hours later

Dare Island: *You good? I'm home.*

ME: *No, I'm not.*

Dare Island: *Talk.*

ME: *I can't. Homework.*

Dare Island: *Don't be like that.*

ME: *Like what? I feel better now. But I won't sometime tomorrow. It always happens like that.*

Dare Island: *Does not talking to me help?*

ME: *No.*

Dare Island: *Ok.*

ME: *I don't know what helps to be honest.*

Dare Island: *Me either.*

ME: *I like writing, and Reba and food. I guess I'm not completely stripped.*

Dare Island: *I'll send you some poems I've written.*

ME: *Sounds interesting.*

I've never received those poems.

November 1, 2013, 10:19 PM

Somehow he would always manage to text me when I was around friends. I'd be sitting in Karen's dorm with our crew Kelly Underwood, Sandra Daniels, and Brady Smokes, and my entire demeanor would change. Either I'd physically, awkwardly re-adjust myself in my seat, or I would blurt out something to the effect of, "oh shit!"

Dare Island: <3

Maybe I blurted an expletive. Karen stole my phone from me, and I fought to get it back again, but Sandra and Brady kept pushing me away. At four against one, I reluctantly gave up and rested assured they wouldn't make it through my lock code. Kelly Googled Reba McEntire's birthday, and Karen correctly guessed the numeric combination. I knew telling Brady that Kelly had a thing for him would come back to bite me in the ass. Oh well. My love life was now in Karen's hands, literally, and I had no control over what was said. All I could do was look pitiful in the corner until they relinquished my phone and I could walk back to my dorm with my head hung in shame. Karen replied through my phone.

Karen: *Fuck you.*
Dare Island: *Just a reminder that you are my friend and I do think of you.*
Karen: *That wasn't a reminder of you thinking of him. That was a reminder of how he'd given you his heart and then you stomped on it until it was shriveled and gross and then left him behind.*
Dare Island: *If he feels that way all he has to do is say so and I can go away.*

I always knew it'd be easy for him.

Karen: *Do you want to go away?*
Dare Island: *I would've already.*
Karen: *That was really vague.*
Dare Island: *Reread it. The answer is no. If I did, I would've already.*
Karen: *See, that's a clearer way of wording it. And he doesn't want you to, but I don't know if it's good for him, honestly. It's pretty much like you're stringing him along at this point and I've been through that*

sort of shit before and I don't want him to have to deal with that because that shit sucks.

He didn't reply, and I made up some excuse to leave. Headache or tired or whatever. I went back to my room and stayed awake for three hours before texting him back how I felt.

ME: *You're not an awful person, though I'm sure you know that. It is okay you don't return the same feelings, it made me really sad for an inordinate amount of time and Karen could see that. Actually, I've been really distant from a lot of my friends lately, but I'm getting off topic. I don't hate you, I love you and I want more than anything for you to be happy. I was just whining for a bit because I knew it wasn't going to be with me, so when you sent me the heart and I showed Karen, she saw how sad it made me and wanted to fix it. Objectively, you should be in my life; you don't throw away five years of friendship and a connection for not-so-fleeting emotions, and I should really grow up. I can't promise you I won't feel bad and you won't be the reason, you will be, but I can ignore the love I have for you and just be there for you as I always have in the past. Only now it is up to you to decide whether or not you would like to be in my life. I love you a lot, Dare. Have a great day, my love.*

Weeks go by and absolutely nothing happened.

November 23, 2013, 1:00 AM

Dare Island: *I'm sorry.*

Again, I was in Karen's dorm. We were watching *Warm Bodies*. When I saw his text I almost cried, and because it hit me out of nowhere I was compelled to exclaim, "shit" again under my breath. It was somber and obdurate, everyone noticed. They asked what was wrong, I said it was nothing or that I died again playing *Temple Run 2*, and they refocused their attention on the movie for a few minutes.

Me: *For what?*

Dare Island: *Everything I did to you.*

Me: *More specific. You didn't do anything. I'm just glad you were in my life.*

Dare Island: *I'm still here.*

Me: *You're in Kentucky. Are you drinking?*

Dare Island: *Duh.*

Me: *That explains it.*

Dare Island: *Nah boo. It's more than that.*

Me: *Then what is it, exactly?*

Dare Island: *Idk. Regret.*

Me: *What do you regret?*

Dare Island: *My treatment of you*

By this time, Karen and the gang deemed my personal life better than the movie. Which it's totally not. *Warm Bodies* is awesome. Once again Karen wrapped her claws around my phone faster than I could say, "Hey bitch, don't wrap your claws around my phone." Karen, like the last time Derek spoke to me, corresponded with him through my phone. I got a new lock code the next day.

Karen: *You damn well should be.*

Dare Island: *Don't worry about me ever talking to you again. If this is what's gonna happen.*

Karen: *Good. You don't deserve the out he gave you. Also, Waldell is completely against me having his phone. He likes to believe that you didn't hurt him, because he likes to pretend he hasn't got a heart. But let's be real, we both know he does. I'm sorry if you don't agree with me, but you don't get to see him when he thinks about you, so I don't think you should get a lot of say in this.*

Dare Island: *K. Bye.*

Reading that last message, Karen gave me back my phone.

Me: *It's me, Dare. She gave me back my phone. I'm sorry. Please talk to me.*

Karen stole my phone again and Brady read that message aloud. They all concluded I was his bottom bitch, basically. I always thought I was more than that. When I made it back to my dorm forty minutes later I messaged him again.

ME: *You know, I'm beginning to think you don't really value my friendship. I think I'm that thing you think about at one am some Friday nights when you're feeling lonely and need some attention.*[19] *The reason why I don't let go of you is because you were a friend of mine and I felt that you cared about my feelings. Am I really just a drunken text message twice a month to you? I think I deserve better. You apologizing was a good start, true. And I realize I was more than eager to roll over and accept it, but what does that exactly say about me? I deserve more than a random Friday night and an overly generalized sweeping apology that doesn't mean shit. When you talk to me, actually talk to me because while you don't want my love, I gave you my friendship and the least you could do is act like you appreciate it. I'm a human being. I am Waldell Goode. I deserve more.*

And somehow thirty minutes later I arrived at...

Me: *I love you. I miss you. I just really wish you'd be my friend again.*

8:50 that evening, basically the next day:

Dare Island: *You know, when I'm sober I physically restrain myself from talking to you. You make it seem like I upset you. When I am drunk that filter weakens. I'm sorry. I do miss you. And when I text you I hope to talk to you, not Karen. I'm sorry.*

Me: *I'm working on getting over my emotions which is upsetting, but nothing hurt worse than when you stopped talking to me. I loved hearing from you and our friendship in general. I felt like you cared about my day and understood the weird things about myself that no one else did, not even me. I thought you wanted to know me, more than others, which was nice... and then I realized you couldn't love me the way I loved you, and I am struggling to accept that every day. But your*

---

[19] It was *always* past midnight on a Friday night.

lack of communication appeared to me as a lack of interest and I felt like you didn't care anymore. So, I reacted and acted out and acted like a child because I still want you. And though I've realized we could never actually be together, I miss the friendship more than anything. That's why I was so desperate to text you after Karen finally gave me my phone back. I miss talking to Dare.

December 24, 2013, 9:30 AM

Dare Island: *Merry Christmas. Happy anniversary lol*
ME: *Thank you. I thought you forgot. Merry Christmas.*

I was in the car listening to Kelly Clarkson's version of "Baby It's Cold Outside," the same song used in *Glee*, which sparked my hate for Ryan Murphy. How cruel a fate he'd text me for the first time in a month and a day while I listened to one of the holiday classics responsible for my personal torment? We didn't speak for nearly three months after that. I thought I was getting better until he left me a voicemail in early March. He didn't say anything of importance, but I loved hearing his voice. Late March, we started speaking again.

March 21, 2014 9:54 AM

Dare Island: *I miss you my friend.*
Me: *I can't talk to you. I still love you. I think about you at some point every day, wishing you'd call, that I'd hear your voice and you'd proclaim your love to me. And I realize that's my fault. I take complete blame for my emotions. It's my responsibility to separate friendship for romantic love. But somewhere back in my head I got the wires crossed and couldn't differentiate between the two. I fucked up. I'm not punishing you or intending to make you feel bad (though it does bring me some joy reading that you miss me). I have come to understand that I'm not the same person I was before last summer. I was fiercely independent, focusing almost solely on my future. A friend of mine told me the other day that you made me human, that you allowed me to remove my mask for a while and reveal that I actually had human*

emotion. Well, I wouldn't necessarily say I've replaced the mask to its proper place, but I am struggling to be myself before you came around and shook things up. It was fun for a while, but you didn't want me back and now I'm processing how to build a bridge and get over it.[20] *But it's hard because you made me acknowledge that you cared about me. I let you influence me in things I shouldn't have; I dreamed of things I knew deep down were never intended for me. So, I kind of have to break myself out of that thinking. It's hard because I still need you, and I certainly want you more than I'm okay with. If I am to truly wish you well I need a longer break from you. I need to not speak with you for a year. There is hurt in my heart that I'm responsible for and you're the trigger. If I am ever going to make it to your wedding and truly wish you and yours the best, I need to conquer whatever the fuck this is making me feel inadequate. I feel that if I can distance myself from you, maybe I can reimagine myself as your friend again. I still feel like shit. I don't want to sacrifice the friendship wholly. I know that I cannot love you like I love you now. I've got to let it go. And I'm sorry, Dare. But I can't hear your fucking name without cringing at the thought of your not loving me back. And I don't know how this works—will it be better if I do not speak to you? I'm sorry. I'm not trying to push you away. I just need you to know that I need this for me. So I can feel like Princess WaWa again and not like your rejection. But if you ever truly need me, I am right here. I'm sorry. I know this is my fault.*

May 21, 2014, 12:03 AM

Me: *Did you ever love me romantically?*
Derek Island: *I will be honest with you and say I did not love, but I did have feelings for you in the romantic way.*

There you have it, my non-love story in what some (namely Karen) would call a fairly melodramatic nutshell. I felt for Derek deeply and he didn't feel back. He couldn't feel back. The joke is on me; all those nights

---

[20] Loretta Keep was all about the building of the bridges.

I didn't sleep for missing him, I silently cried for him, I walked away from public situations for my own sanity, I continued giving him fragments of myself he never asked for, pieces he flat out rejected, and I have never even kissed him. He's never wanted to kiss me. Twisted isn't it? Or at least a little fucked up. I've spent the better portion of life guarding myself, hoping I would never have to feel anything just to have Sandra Daniels look me in the eye one day and tell me, "He made you a person. I have so many saved messages from you about last summer. You said you were 'giddy.' It was like Waldell without the mask. Something I've never seen in real life." I've come to find I don't like being that. I've grown fond of the bitch within—how upsetting when the bitch would all but vanish whenever I'd get a message from the almighty Derek. I wasn't fair to myself. I should've tried harder to block access from his advances. I tried so hard to be superhuman, and I failed.

I blocked Derek on Facebook for nearly two months starting on February 7, 2014. We had gone one month without speaking; it was a decision I had to make to grow and move on from him and all the unsettled strife he caused me. He hadn't a clue we weren't speaking anymore, didn't notice my absence from his life. I thought that was okay. That his forgetting me was the best thing I could use to remind myself I was never important to him, and I needed that time to make myself stronger.

One evening in March, I lay in bed texting or surfing the Internet, when he phoned me. I didn't answer. I froze. I texted Karen about what I should do, her response was, "Only speak with him if you think you can handle it." I listened to his voicemail three times. "I miss you, friend. Wanted to talk to you about my life recently..." Hearing his voice was like biting into your first piece of chocolate after resisting carbs for seventy-five days.

I waited an hour before calling him back. It was already two a.m. when he called, and I really didn't want to speak with him unless I had to. The satisfaction of his phone going to voicemail overtook me so greatly, my heart raced as a criminal's would, narrowly missing the bullet of a sharpshooter. His voicemail was exceedingly well balanced in comparison to the one I left him back in November of 2013. I don't remember it, but according to my roommate it went a little like: "Fuck you, 'cause you made me love you, and I never thought I'd be able to let anyone in." Sounds like me.

Lone voicemail aside, it took Derek until April 13, 2014 to realize we weren't Facebook friends. Forthwith, sending that last text on March 21, 2014, I felt better. I no longer held a grudge toward him, definitely not in the same way. One morning mid-April we began texting, he asked me why I was suddenly ready to talk to him, and my reply was, "I woke up and realized I was over you." I can truly say I am, as much as I can be. I have told anyone who asks why I message Derek now; I would rather wake up and find my pinky finger missing than find Derek Island in my bed. We just don't belong together. I accept that fact. I wish him nothing but the best. And it is a little weird, but re-friending someone in real life is a much lengthier process than it is on Facebook. I will *never* attend his wedding. I do will wish him well, and mean it from the bottom of my heart. The whole pinky thing might be a little harsh, but I'm done trying to force someone to want me.

That doesn't mean I don't still mourn. Derek's heart was broken by someone else out in Kentucky. He texted me this while I was in class one day, confessing the guy played with his mind and chose someone else over him. As Professor Wilson wrapped up my Virginia Woolf lecture course, I worked tediously to contain myself, inwardly pleading for dismissal. As soon as she released us, I reared back my head and laughed so hard I almost cried, and my ribs ached. I couldn't stop laughing until I made it to work ten minutes later, and when I finally took a moment to catch my breath, I instantaneously felt like shit. I was finding amusement in someone else's misery. That wasn't me. That's not what I do, and it wasn't okay. I wasn't raised that way. I believe in karma; I'm a Christian and I'm a *person.* I am a person whether I like it or not, and I have no right to treat people like they are less than. I bottled my nasty contempt for love and did what I do best. I was there for him in spite of myself.

History repeating itself, being there for Derek consisted of listening to all the sappy songs he posted on my wall or his social media page. It's his pain. It wasn't one of Whitney Houston's or Mariah Carey's ballads he pinned that time. He went with Amber Riley's "Colorblind." I saw he shared it with me when I woke up that Tuesday afternoon before my classes. I almost ignored it, quickly resolving that if I was going to allow Derek back in my life I had to fully invest in being his friend again, including indulging in his questionable musical tastes. I clicked the play button. Three minutes into the song I was choking back tears. Having voiced every devastating wound I'd felt for eight months up until then, I put the song on repeat and went through my day on autopilot. This wasn't happening because I missed Derek. I didn't want him back and was not yearning for his adoration. I missed the *joie de vivre* that unrequited love stole from me.

For months I painted vacant smiles on my face, deceit blossomed in my eyes, and unmentionable sorrow weighed my soul. Nothing felt as uniquely brilliant as the years before I gave my heart away only to have it stamped "return to sender." I didn't want Derek, or to hug anyone or laugh or be comforted. I wanted to cry and scream and bitch and yell because I was slowly dying inside, and how can you tell someone you're unsettled by a person you never even kissed? How do you speak of such pain and not sound like a buffoon? How do you not feel like one? How do you retrieve what you lose when you give your heart away and discover no one wanted it? I don't want Derek back; nevertheless, I do long for that innocence a broken heart strips you of when you aren't prepared for complete and total devastation. I was destroyed in some catastrophically emotional way, and now the rebuilding begins.

I haven't given up on love; that would be easier. I'll never say this out loud, but I still want someone who's right for me. That scares me. I've learned I don't trust easily. I think about men, I think about my father and how men cheat, how my mother's life utterly went up in flames at the will of my father, and I renounce men at all costs. Except for Karen's dad, but those are two previous chapters.

I was walking around on campus one night playing Pandora on my iPhone the first time I heard Boyce Avenue's cover of "A Thousand Miles," originally written and performed by Vanessa Carlton. The university looked as it always had. Christmas lights were artfully draped around imported trees that grew along the red and white cobblestone walkways leading up to the colonial style library and academic buildings, the temperature appeasingly seventy degrees or so, and when I looked up, I could still see some stars shining through the thick blanket of night and light pollution. I love it when I can see stars at nighttime. Something about it felt superior and unfathomably paradisiacal. The stars' incandescence mixed with the magical luster of stillness perpetuated the sentiment of God's dream. This was how nights were supposed to feel. I was alone and it didn't bother me. I did ponder what it would be like having someone walking alongside me, slipping their hand through mine, stopping to stare at me because I was there, or gently kissing me out of wanting to. That wasn't the case, I was alone. And I danced by myself on an abandoned campus under the glimmer of the night sky and twinkling strings of lights anyway. I am single. That doesn't mean I'm any less whole.

There are stories I could tell, horrible Grindr anecdotes that would shock even the kinkiest of gay black men from Farmville, Virginia. Guys who think I'm a woman, or beg me to be more masculine. Guys who are either interested in a gym buddy or part time "tranny" for play. I am neither of those things. Part of the reason I fell for Dare is because he realized that about me. And Sandra's observation retains its applicability. I am a person. I have thoughts and desires, wants and wishes, and I'm nobody's fetish. Trans activist, Janet Mock once said in an interview "I have someone who loves and I'm lucky to have him, but he's lucky to have me as well." I have to believe there is someone who will love me for being myself. Derek, bless his heart, wasn't that person. I'm sure he tried his hardest. I have to continue believing I deserve a love story and I am worthy of having one. It would be nice to find someone who loves you back. Lord knows I don't know what that's like.

And even still if that never happens, just like before I'm sure I will find myself dancing any fucking way.

Twenty: Mother

Senior year I went to prom with my friend Morgan Deathbox and split the tab for professional prom photos. I forgot all about them by the end of the evening. We went back to a friend's place and I got smashing drunk on hard iced tea, no less. A year later on summer break from university, I met up with Morgan and we spent several weeks reminiscing about our tragic high school days, looking through photos before discovering the lost prom of 2012. Taking the embarrassing reminders home, I blew up one of the pocket sized photos, put it into an eight-by-eleven frame, and set it on an end table in my mother's living room. My stepfather commented on the enticing allure of Megan's legs, her royal purple gown having a split running up to her knee, and when I half-jokingly mentioned to my mother that Wilbert was ogling my then eighteen-year-old friend, we laughed it off before she settled in for the night and I went back to secluding myself in the wonderful world of the Internet. And everything was fine, I thought. That was the night my mother killed my stepfather.

Not quite. It should be noted she does suspiciously partake in watching her fair share of *Snapped.*

That was the night I knew my mother wasn't going to get any better.

Seven months after my mother's accident in January, I fought to ignore my parents' arguing by popping in my headphones and turning up whichever program I sought to binge watch that summer. For 2013 it was *Dawson's Creek.* Joey and Pacey's trite teen schmaltz paled in comparison to the war being waged before my shifting eyes. Nothing I did could drown out their sonorous yelling, or my mother's acidic invectives and my stepfather's insufficient deflections.

The debacle began with them in their room located in the back of our one-story rental home. Our house was a beautiful redbrick, green shutter home—small with a lot of personality; some would call it "cozy." It's the type of home you'd expect your grandmother to live in, with curtains draped from every window and the aroma of freshly baked cookies permanently emanating from the white walls decorated with pictures from all your soccer games and school accomplishments. When you visited, you knew every memory would be hung with care and you'd gain at least five pounds from the scent of fattening goodies alone.

The reality was, behind the closed green door on Crestview Drive surrounded by oblong hedges, friendly neighbors, a backyard full of trees, and an easy walk down the path to the podunk town of Farmville, lay a far less glamorous and highly demented production of *Who's Afraid of Virginia Woolf.* They went off script and improvised a little, but Mother and Wilbert Eames' efforts were as unwavering and dedicated as Ms. Taylor's and Mr. Burton's enactments. All the cynical bravado a tumultuous marriage can afford you really can result in the role of a lifetime, no matter how much it eats at those around you and at the core of your own humanity. In her drunken ramblings and incoherent spiteful abasements, deep down, rested my mother's true nature. Since 2006, I've learned the many ways a few too many bottles of wine can dilute the soul.

The night proceeded as usual. Wilbert escaped my mother's room looking for peace blocked off in his den. The grandmother who occupied the residence before we moved in had the garage converted into another sitting area. Wilbert claimed it as his personal space, and my mother ignored him. Never gave a shit about it. It was her home too. She didn't get her own personal space.

They took a detour, moving away from the den, and made their way into the kitchen, doing a huge disservice to the *Dawson's Creek* finale I was watching at the kitchen table. Something inconceivable happened with the Pacey/Joey/Dawson love triangle and I had no idea why James Van Der Beek was sobbing so fervidly. He was always such a pretty crier.

I think Wilbert moved the argument in there to show me. I think he wanted help defending himself. I think he wanted me to calm my mother down. I think he wanted me to insert myself into her line of fire. I think he didn't want to be berated like he was the stepchild and she the parent. I think he just wanted help.

I think this because he, in the middle of the argument, stopped to look me in the eye and ask, "Can't you just help me?"

I averted my eyes from his, permitting no passage of time before deflectingphone, "Nope, that is *your* wife." I was across the room with my headphones in, staring intently at the computer screen, sitting at the dining room table. I knew that would have been enough distance from the action if this was an ordinary tiff in the middle of the day; tonight mom was in overdrive.

"You're a fat ugly bastard!" "I'm more attractive than you anyway!" "You are fat and ugly and stupid!" "I'm going to leave your ass!" The person I referenced earlier was becoming harder and harder to salvage. What happens when a bottle dissolves a person's core altogether? As much as I wanted to ignore it and pretend my mother was my stepfather's issue alone, it wasn't funny anymore, or a nondescript ordeal that could easily be disregarded as "nothing." Her problem was going to kill her, and for all Wilbert's faults he never deserved to be spoken to like a moronic simpleton

I'd written chapter six three months before, shared it with my youth pastor Tom, my two older sisters, and Derek, all of whom concluded it would have been a categorically atrocious idea to give my mother the confessional and it wouldn't help anything. I thought it best to listen to my elders and recommitted to waiting until I was financially independent before directly addressing my mom's illness with the woman herself.

On the morrow, I took a breather. I walked around my home and dealt with the romantic trifles obviously solvable in my mind. Yes, Joey and Pacey were at it again, so much that they edged the title character out of his own eponymous TV drama. Poor Dawson. Life in a dated teen soap is a bitch.

Every now and again, when the WiFi ceased working properly or I had to wait for Netflix to load, I'd take a few minutes to perambulate around the house as if I was a voyeur appraising the property. There's not much to do in Farmville a year post high school graduation, not that high school was a parade of endless drunken parties. The only ones worth remembering were always Karen's, and they were largely familial occasions for just about every Caucasian "talented and gifted" or "honors" student and their parents, and every goddamn Filipino in the tri-state area. But oh my God the *food*! I kind of want to cry thinking about her mom's egg rolls and creamy leche flan. Every July Fourth I like to throw down and they expect me to. The Anghels offered me a real sense of home, of family.

Where was I? Oh, perambulation and such. The living room was the single newly decorated area in the house since my leaving for university. My mother tried her best to make the space most comfortable for Wilbert, me, and my sisters. We didn't have much, and multiple times in my youth I found myself without a bed. I've slept on the floor, couch cushions, a cot, and an infinite number of blow-up mattresses. One of her first decisions when they moved in this house was to purchase me a queen-sized bed. Living with two sisters, I usually got the short end of the stick when it came to habitation. We were clearly moving on up; our living room had brown leather couches the ones like in Cann's house, mahogany end tables, lamps, and curtains. It was very different from the furnitureless duplex apartment we lived in for two and a half years before making the move to an actual house.

Complete with this new living room came developed photos on the wall. Wilbert never liked hanging photos, fearing probable wall damage, but since the wall already had pre-embedded nails when we moved in, he let it slide. It's kinda funny; he keeps thinking he's the man of the house. Everyone knows my mother is.

On the wall surrounded by the numerous photos was an image of my mother's deceased cousin and her daughter, who was an infant when her mother passed. It was one of those side-by-side photos, half was the mother around age seventeen, and half was the daughter around age seventeen. Erika is the mother's name. I think she was in her mid-to-late twenties when she passed. Cocaine addiction. Everyone knew, and no one wanted to say anything. Too touchy to talk about. Too dreary to address. Too painful to acknowledge, so why bring it up? My mother often said that was an oversight in her family: no one wanted to talk about anything. Erika died in my great aunt's arms, and Cherokee had to grow up without a mother. Seeing that, I took a breath and walked into Wilbert's sacred den, requesting use of his printer he established solely for work purposes. I told him it was important information I had to print off from university, and reluctantly the unshakable shook.

My mother came home that evening while I was cleaning out the refrigerator. Wilbert and my mother worked so often there wasn't anyone who'd perform the major cleaning jobs. I returned from school agreeing to do the bigger projects, or I was bribed with money from my mom. I sealed chapter six in an envelope and labeled it "Mother."

As she walked through the kitchen door, I stopped what I was doing and asked, "Hey Mom, how are you?" She looked at the flat, pale Pandora's box I clutched in my hand, asking me what it was. "Just read it." I urged her, and returned to the refrigerator. She opened it right there and read the entire chapter. I thought it would take her a minute; I thought she would leave the room. She stood in the same spot motionless for fifteen minutes, reading the chapter that revealed everything.

"Be sure to scrub inside the meat compartment," and she addressed nothing else. She folded the chapter back and looked at me with tears in her eyes. She pulled me in with outstretched arms, and like the bitch I am inside I cried wonderfully miserable rivers of agony.

"I'm so sorry." I sobbed. I always cry the hardest at the most random occasions, like when Diamond graduated university.

"It's fine. You told the truth." Her voice was surprisingly calm. A tear ran down her face.

"I just always hear how you talk about Erika, and that nobody wanted to mention anything before it was too late," I droned on.

"I know. It's okay," she said. She continued to hug me for a minute before she left the room and said she was going to bed. I resumed cleaning the refrigerator. Clorox and tears, my favorite cleaning solution. I felt things were going to get better. She was going to rehab.

She got drunk that night.

Just like the night before, I was sitting in the kitchen with *Joey's Creek*[21] when my mother hastily intruded. She was in a nightgown with a red Solo cup in her hand, I assume contained Woodbridge. She was a tad too coherent for it to be anything brown. "You know, I wasn't always like this." She slurred. "I can be better. I didn't drink in my twenties. I'm sorry I was a bad mom."

"You aren't a bad mom. I have a great life." It was never my goal to make her feel guilty.

"And you, you have nobody there for you."

"What are you talking about?"

"At your school, you were so happy you had no one there to clap for you."

"Oh..."

"You know how that feels, to know that your child would rather be alone instead of have you there because I work? That doesn't make any sense. I would have cheered for you if you wanted me to be there."

"Mom, I know."

"But I'm such an evil bitch for working. You know why I work?"

"Because you have to..." This drunk was different from all the other ones.

---

21 Dawson was barely a part of the show at that point.

"And I love Amethyst, but she was a tough child. But she has a better heart out of all of you. I know I can always come to her if I need anything."

"That's true, Mom."

"She's so good. I never wanted to hurt her. She'll always be there. *Always*. And you say life kicked his ass. He kicked his own ass." I knew whom she meant. I nod, the only moment my body permitted me.

"Do you know what it's like to have your husband touch your child?"

I had to take a second. My mother, who's always had a towering presence in my life, looked like the defenseless child we all must secretly really be.

"No, ma'am."

"He was my best friend. My soulmate. I thought we were going to spend the rest of our lives together."

"Oh." What else could I say?

"And I couldn't protect my child. Do you know how what feels as a mother to not be able to do the one thing you're supposed to do?" I got up from the table and walked over to her standing in the door frame. I hugged her, and she wept on my shoulder. A few seconds passed before she pulled away. "And I tried getting therapy for us, for all of us, but when your dad went to jail he lost his job and his benefits. I was only working part time then, and the state wouldn't pay for it 'cause when I asked they said it shouldn't have been so traumatic because there wasn't penetration." She sniffled some more. "And they judged me. My brother called from Maryland and proposed he take Diamond because 'you don't break up a home.' What kind of bullshit was that? Was I supposed to wait until he touched my other daughter?"

"Uh... I... don't know."

"But life kicked his ass. He kicked his own ass."

"You're right."

"But I will try to be better. I promise."

"Okay. That is enough." And then she wished me good night and stumbled back to her room. It was already around eleven p.m., and the strangest part for me centered around who to confide in. There was Derek and his aching desire, "let me care!" I think I attempted calling or texting Pop. The resolution was simpler than I was making it; I walked the short hallway to my room and called Karen.

"Hey!" she whispered. "Is everything okay? I'm with the kids out in the living room."

"Um, I'm fine. I just gave my mother her chapter and it was kind of heavy."

"Oh, are you okay?"

"Yeah, I'm fine. Go back to bed."

"You sure?"

"Yes I'm sure! Thank you, though."

"All right love, goodnight."

"Good night, Karen. Love you."

"Love you too."

To my bewilderment, not everyone has undergone epiphanic episodes with their alcoholic mother. I was alone for this one. I finally tried to let someone else in, and now maybe I'm too far gone to ever master that practice. For all my writing, I've never quite conquered communicating. That night, I had a breakthrough of my own. As I lay in bed replaying the day's events, I sent Derek this text message:

Me: *I just had an orgasm of the heart. I was lying in bed praying to God for courage today in giving my mother her chapter. I began thinking about my future and why I want five kids, and the things I'd want to do differently, showering them with love. Then I did something I always do. I prayed for love. Whereas normally it is a general statement or I'm praying for you, Pop, Karen etc, I prayed for myself and I started crying. That was the first time I had ever prayed for love explicitly for myself. It was my first time stating that I need, deserve and want love, and it was more cathartic than thirteen chapters of teenage indignation. I feel like my soul has flushed ten years of backed-up fluid. There is power in prayer and though I've tempted to put others' hearts above my own, mine matters too. It's sort of a free and beautiful feeling to wash over you, Dare. And I'm glad I've gotten to share it with you! Have a great day, hun. I'm rooting for you!*

In a way I can't explicate, I was open in ways I wasn't open before.

I'd like to say after that evening my mother stopped drinking. I can't. I'd like to say after our conversation, my mother stopped drinking as heavily. I don't know. One break from school I came home, she looked healthier. She had listed on a bucketlist her plan to lose weight and to travel and celebrate life more. A few months later I was away at CNU and picked up twenty dollars she sent me through Walmart. When I called to thank her, she drawled in a slurred voice.

"KnowIAlwaysLoveYou. NoMatterWhatHappens, IAlwaysLoveYou."
That is the truth I have to accept. My mother has a disease. It isn't going
to be easy.

I try my best not to judge my mother. I never want to live the life she
lived or endure that level of betrayal. I can't trust men because I think
they will all turn out to be my father. I'm afraid to drink because I think
I'll turn into my mother, or worse, make a mistake like my father did
that abhorrent night fifteen years ago. I'll still take a drink, but I know
when I need to stop. Four shots and I'm gone. Seriously, don't let me
have any more unless I gain weight or hit a growth spurt. I still date men.
I may have to text Karen their name, address, license plate, phone
number, and picture before going out, but that's just dating in the
twenty-first century. I have to keep my mind open and my heart free or
else I will not be living at all. I am not my mother. I am not going to
marry my father. Their lives are not mine; I have no claim to them, and
I won't claim them. I love the life my parents gave us: Diamond's getting
her master's, Amethyst's working and in school for her bachelor's, and I
graduate Christopher Newport University in six months. Our family has
seen its fair share of tragedy, and yet we're still here. Diamond and my
mother lived through the worst moments in their lives with dignity and
grace, and I will forever stand in awe of my mother's light in our darkest
moments. We didn't have everything; things were tight for a while and
we've all had to resort to student loans, but we've always had each other.
My mother always worked, and I've always had my sisters before anyone
else in the world.

I think this is a success story. There's so much more love than there
is clinical psychology. Compared to the way our lives could have gone, if
she let the others judge her and she stayed with my father, I think what
a dark life that could have been and how we would have never recovered.
I would have never spoken to my parents again, and we would have been
broken beyond repair. Nothing could have fixed us. For all her faults,
her imperfections, witticisms, anecdotes, wisdom, flaws, beauty,
intelligence, kindness, sarcasm, cash, and resilience, I thank God for my
mother and I thank God she's always been there for me, even when I
grew up to be the most beautiful daughter she never had. It takes a real
mother to love her cross-dressing gay son anyway.

Twenty-One: Where the Fuck Are They Now

Tyler Paulson's dream lasted for one semester before he realized he couldn't afford Annette Bening's alma mater. He was evicted from campus and lived homeless for a few months before flying back to Virginia. He remained with Andrea, and they are moving into their first apartment together one hour out from Chesterfield, Virginia, where my mother and stepfather relocated to after he retired as a state trooper of over thirty years. My fear of never seeing Tyler again now seems as ridiculous as the notion that my life was over because I couldn't go to the private out-of-state college I wanted to. Tyler Paulson will forever be in my life, even if we're not as close as we were in ninth grade. People grow and change, and that's fine. He's hotter now. He is living with no regrets, and I shall continue to strive to be more like him.

My father's girlfriend died two days before I could get to her and say goodbye. She took her last breath the day before Easter Sunday 2013. Her funeral was dignified and traditionally Baptist, and I mourned for her son and those she left behind. It made me happy that her family acknowledged my father and his part in nursing Wendy through her final hours, ensuring she was comfortable when she finally heard Jesus calling her name. Wendy was only in her forties, and the funeral had to occur within a week because though she stopped breathing, the cancer continued to eat through her body post-mortem. Her son said it was one of her final wishes to be cremated, which occurred quickly following the open casket memorial. I assume she's with him now or riding the tide in the Atlantic Ocean.

I didn't know what to expect when it came to my father's health after she died. He was distraught. Wendy was one of the more devastating deaths he'd felt. His best friend and soulmate died a couple years before. At fifty, he's at a crucial time in life, finding that a substantial amount of people he's loved in this world are now in another one. That's an enduring pain I hope to never feel at such magnitude. I don't agree with my father most of the time. I don't like the way he lives his life or his defeatist attitude that haunts his every move at this age. He hurt Diamond, and I don't know if I can ever forgive him for that, but the way he cared for Wendy in her last days showed me what it means to be a strong black man. Is he redeemed? Massaging Wendy's feet and cleaning her stool aren't acts done for admiration; they are performed out of humility and love. I don't get to decide who's a good person, but thinking of my father and Wendy's last years, there is a chance for my papa. I hope. I have to believe that. He is my father. I have no other real options. Whenever I think of him I never know how to feel. You tell me.

Cann has fallen in love and has been in a stable relationship for over a year. A match made in lesbian heaven, I'm assuming, instead of the pearly gates one would enter through the cervix. What the fuck? It was me and her alone and bitter in high school, and she got out and found love, and is perfectly content. It was her who got both dreams, not Tyler Paulson. In her second year at Smith, Cann was awarded the Jeanne McFarland Prize for excellence in the study of women and gender, and the Thomas Corwin Mendenhall Prize for excellence in history. I remain jealous of her in the best way. One day I pray to retain half as much knowledge and integrity as she. If there is anyone worthy of a happy ending, it would be Cann. She is the soul with the burden of perpetual luminosity to bear, living in a world still trying to unlock the voluminous mysteries that lie just underneath that carefully untamed crop of lesbian-conforming hair follicles sprouting from her scalp. I still can't believe she's a butch. Or that she once called me Gay Lord.

Karen's parents are absolutely fabulous, and I thank God every day they are in my life. The last time I saw her father, he came up to move Karen out of her dorm for summer break. I left my coat at my father's place. Karen let me borrow one of hers for the day. It was one of those black double-breasted trench style jackets she knew looked better on me. I knew she knew it, but she'd never say it. We went to eat at a Chinese place near campus, and he yelled at me for not ordering enough food. My cream cheese wontons magically transformed into General Tso's chicken at his expense. I discovered his love for soul music, and we recreated all the ballads my parents forced upon me ever since my adolescent auricles developed into adult-sized ears. We took turns singing *Reasons* by Earth Wind and Fire, and performing an impromptu duet of "Endless Love." Guess who was Diana! We went to see *The Other Woman* starring Cameron Diaz and Leslie Mann, not the depressing one with Natalie Portman and Lisa Kudrow, and when he managed to pack Karen's oversized dorm room in his 2002 Ford Explorer after over ninety minutes of strategizing (it was an astounding feat, I applauded when he able to shut the latch to the trunk), we took pictures before he drove off. I was with Karen, her youngest sibling Mikele, and her father on the best send-off of the year. As I shift through the photos one by one on my iPhone, it's nice to know you can have more than one true family.

I got a text from her mom today urging that I check my email. She sent me an advertisement for Cher's latest concert. How fitting was it that she unwittingly assisted me in answering Cher's crucial question? Jennifer Anghel always rooted and dreamt for me. She and Johanson and Mrs. Lupas, and so many more. I've been unreasonably blessed with all the mothers in my life. I can never, ever place them over my own, but wow, when I think of all the love they've shared and how many times they've advised me, fed me, directly financed me, indirectly clothed me (in my closet there are two sets of clothes, one is mine and one is Karen's). I am only as grateful as my heart is strong. The many times I thought I'd flatlined, they were there first on the scene to resuscitate, and like they say, "the beat goes on."

Their stories don't get the bleak tales and dark revelations at eleven p.m. They were never meant to. A mother's relationship with her gay son is complex and fettered and imperfect and trying. God makes it this way so their story can have substantial meaning and depth beyond reproach.

Within hours of seeing *Frozen,* Karen came out as pansexual-ish. Or, kinda straight and "more interested in who a person is rather than what they look like." She must've really had something she needed to let go of. She carried Jeremiah with her for a long time, and I thought that story would have a better ending. There was definitely a need for closure on her end, and I was hoping she'd get it. Why couldn't Jeremiah just love her? She's beautiful and smart and funny, and could use someone for all those lonely periods no one ever wants to talk about. Or if he couldn't love her, why not say it so we all can move the fuck on? Not everyone is Derek Island and has a flair for romanticized endings, and it took a few ugly days and a few "I'm not going to think about it" and "I don't want to hear his fucking name" days until she posted on Tumblr and found Shooter. He's short with brown hair and glasses, and they talk all the fucking time. Like the second amendment-supporting friend I am, I met him, introduced myself, and then promptly threatened to kill him. [22]

I've been overly involved with Karen's love life for years. I would stop and ask every attractive male with a decent personality if they were into Asians, and show them a good cleavage picture of my good ole Catholic friend. This has been my practice since eleventh grade. I had a dream senior year of high school that she fell in love with Paul, a pretty boy with green eyes and medium athletic build one year our junior who had plans on attending Harvard. (Waitlisted. He's still a rich white man. Here's hoping something in his life will go right.) In my dreary reverie, I told our friend Johnny I was upset because I don't think she'll need me anymore. I woke up to texts informing me that Karen had no intentions of being with Paul, and my neurotic behavior superseded the bounds of consciousness.

Flash forward two years later, and here's this motherfucker threatening to take her away from me. I have to trust her; the way I see it, she's officially a twenty-one-year-old adult, and I have to respect her wishes and the man in her life. Or I'm at least supposed to try to. This is new for me. I'm used to boundaries being merely a suggestion.

I had another dream a few days ago. We were back in a high school dungeon being taught by a vampire, in some weird, nightmarish comedic intersection of *Penny Dreadful, True Blood,* and *Wizards of Waverly Place.* Karen told me she was dying. We all knew she was dying, and she was at peace with it. When I tried talking to her, she said earnestly, "I don't want she to seek treatment. This way my final days won't drag on."

I did what came naturally to me; I smiled in her face, "I respect your wishes. I will do anything in my power to make your death as comfortable as possible." Skeptically, she turned her back and I began diligently working for a cure.

There was even an escape from vamp camp in order to make a deal with werewolves who drank heavily in a nearby bar. Don't know what I was aiming for there, no stone could be unturned or un-smashed, and researched for its life-saving acuity. Plus bears are kinda my thing, and

---

[22] They have since amicably split. I had nothing to do with it, I swear.

I think Grindr led me there to the wolf men. I landed in the middle of a brawl and was close to being dog food before Sandra Daniels, Karen's roommate in real life and the dream, swooped in to save me.

Flustered, like a mom finding her toddler attempting to fork the outlet, she found my eyes. "You're about to do something stupid."

We began talking about why I put my life in danger and how I have to accept Karen's choices. Dream Sandra told me, "Waldell, you can't control her death like you tried controlling her love life."

Dream Waldell took a second, considered her statement, and responded caringly with, "The hell I can't!" The next morning, or evening-morning, whatever that is in vampire land, I told Karen where I got all the scars and wounds on my body and I told her I wasn't ready for her to die. She saw how greatly it affected me, and agreed to review more treatments for her illness. Then I think the rapture happened.

That afternoon when I woke up for realzies I texted Karen to make sure she was still alive. Regrettably for my closet, she still was. I don't know what that delusion should have symbolized or alluded to—I'm not that neurotic control freak who thinks they need to save the world even when they are instructed not to. I think it could've meant I'm the chosen one to single-handedly stop the rapture. Am I the second coming of Jesus Christ? 'Cause that would've been fly as hell to note on my birth certificate.

Our friendship could never be summed up in the pages of some pretentious, self-indulgent bildungsroman. As every coming-of-gay story needs, she's the sanity to my bedazzled confusion. That day her father picked her up for summer break, I hugged Mikele and Pete goodbye and told them I loved them. Karen and I had to walk back to her dorm to return the moving cart and retrieve her ID from the front desk.

We walked through light rain staving off feelings, like we've learned oh so well to do after years with one another. We're not Kurt and Rachel from *Glee* for crying out loud! The night was pretty with a few stars peeking out past bluish gray rain clouds. I looked at her and then briskly looked away.

"Karen, you know how I feel about you." This part is icky.

"I know, Waldell. You don't have you to say it."

I looked to the sky, the rain a cool refreshment from such a Hallmark moment. "Thank God!"

"You tell me every time you get drunk... and just so you know, I love you too." We giggled because this was always awkward and weird. We're normally robots around each other. Bitchy, catty, slapping, punching robots. Bitch technically means "I love you," now. We got to the front door of her dorm and hugged one another for the last time that academic year. Just as I was about to pull away and turn to leave, she stopped me. Contorting her face to resemble her mother's exactly, Karen refused to let me leave without one last demand: "Bitch, give me back my coat."

Enough with that bitch, on to God now. I am a deeply flawed human being. God loves me anyway. I don't know what a perfect Christian is, and I surely don't want to meet that person. Does God care about language? Probably not. Does God care if I wear nail polish? Does that make me Hitler or a rapist? I can't really see it. God cares who we are more than how we look on the outside. What would He/She care if we prefer 'darn' to 'damn.' These matters are trivial. I've always had anointing in my life and God has a plan for me, particularly when I don't understand it at all. I've wasted time mad at Her for not finding a way for me to attend that fancy private out-of-state college—I wasn't aware what a blessing it was to go to university with my best friend and be there for my father when Wendy passed. I don't know where or when or how; one day I will see God's plan and I will pray with all my might not to fuck it up.

Derek and I have remained friends. I was chatting with a friend when it hit me he's been the only consistent gay man in my life other than RuPaul. Pop is bi. Latesa, a real friend of mine who has witnessed the Derek saga first hand, shared her view that one day the stars will align for me and Derek when we get our shit together. I laughed and said that'd be like buying a ticket aboard the Titanic post the infamous iceberg crash. I'm no Kate Winslet. Platonic distance it is.[23]

I never did locate one impressive sexual partner. The whole Derek crisis changed things. I need more than a one evening sexcapade. It's easy to slip up with Grindr and OkCupid and every other penis-seeking app in the palm of your hand. It's hard believing I am worth more than an anonymous ejaculation and it took Derek's rebuffing me to see that.

---

[23] It's in the realm of possibility I'll get drunk and want to sleep with him. I'm not perfect, and it will never happen anyway.

Guys should think more of me than the condom they come in. Oh, and I'm still a virgin depending on who you ask.

I look back over this thing I wrote and it's interesting to think about the people who didn't get a chapter. Why wasn't Mrs. Lupas prominently featured? She's the closest thing I've got to Maya Angelou. Where are the memories of dancing along to Britney Spears with my sisters in the midst of my parents' divorce? Shouldn't my father get his own chapter? Why did my mother get three? And how the hell were Karen's parents incorporated in so many? And my sister Amethyst, she's the single greatest person alive—the banana to my split, the Gina to my Pam, the Tracy Turnblad to my Penny Pingleton—she got nothing. Her story is much larger than I could ever try delineating in any of these passages. She's favorite character, long-running sitcom material. I couldn't tell her story without it completely overshadowing my own. I would've done her a disservice, truthfully. Diamond my oldest sister, Athena my youngest, there's no explanation. They are more a part of me than I could ever think about. If they ever disappeared from my life, I'd have *nothing*. Who knows why these stories came to me the way they did, and about who they chose to reflect. At this run-in of my life, their stories are my stories, and maybe one day I'll have it in me to tell even more. I thank Tyler, Wendy, Cann, Derek, the Anghels, and my mother for their lives and living and dying so uniquely. I would not have my own story if I did not also have theirs. That is the single most important invention isn't it? The sharing of stories.

Twenty-Two: Trayvon Martin

On July 13, 2013, OWN premiered a comedy special, *Herlarious,* hosted by Wanda Sykes, featuring several other notable and amateur comics. Having always been a huge fan of OWN and its female-driven, life-affirming programming, I prepared to lavishly indulge myself while laughing my ass off in my stepfather's empty den. This was before he retired and on that particular evening he worked the late shift. I had the only room with a decent sized television and sitting area to myself until eleven p.m. God was working in my favor. An hour before the event, I ran across the street to Sheetz to purchase dinner for that night: a twelve-inch cold-cut sub made-to-order, complete with tomatoes, lettuce, onions, and bacon that cost about a dollar extra. I also had to have mozzarella sticks, a sixteen-ounce Coke in a *glass* bottle, and a miniature bag of chocolate covered pretzels. When I do OWN specials, I do them big.

As I sat there watching Ms. Sykes make a comical ass of herself, my thoughts subsided and the world seemed a little less like a superimposing sphere of pervasive confinement. I was only mildly entertained, and the humor was inoffensive enough. It had a broad appeal to women of all ages and their families. Wanda Sykes on OWN couldn't be Wanda Sykes on HBO. Good for OWN. I was snuggly comfortable in my Snuggie with virtually no other plans on a Saturday night; I was going to enjoy the show for what it was worth. With all that food and serenity, how could things go wrong?

July 13, 2013, 10:13 PM

Cann: *I AM SO FUCKING DONE WITH AMERICA RIGHT NOW.*
Me: Orange is the New Black?

We'd been watching that show and texting about the episodes, like a Netflix book club.

Cann: *George Zimmerman was found not guilty.*

I didn't have the slightest clue who the fuck George Zimmerman was. I wasn't following the case. It didn't appear there was anything I could contribute to the argument. Unarmed African-American kid shot to death by a neighborhood watch member after said member was instructed not to pursue said African-American kid by the cops twice. There's an abundance of misery in the world—I try to block it out the best I can. I couldn't any longer for Cann's sake, my well-informed Caucasian friend. I, on the other hand, was an African-American kid who just wore a hoodie and walked to the 24-hour convenience store close to home late at night to buy candy. To adequately respond to Cann's text, I first had to Google George Zimmerman.

Cann: *Everything is fucked up.*
Me: *It is. I didn't even pay close attention to the case because I thought it was shut as soon as it was opened. Yet another shitty verdict by a more than questionable justice system.*
Cann: *The United States Justice System (and the United States) is racist. There is no argument to convince otherwise. I'm so done. I can't imagine how you feel.*

I didn't know how to feel. I had to feel for her first.

Me: *I feel like the United States revealed itself, and I am shocked. I have no delusions otherwise.*
Cann: *You're right. I wish there was something we could do.*
ME: *Yeah. America.*
Cann: *How do we even survive here? How did Angela Davis and Harvey Milk and all the rest get the nerve and the strength?*
Two minutes later, Cann: *sorry. Emotion.*
Me: *I don't even know. They believed in America. They believed in a dream or a promise and I'm willing to wager such feats are preordained; I just don't know what to believe in anymore.*
Cann: *What do we believe in? I mean this is a world that would prefer us dead.*

Me: *Well, me dead and you silent.*

Cann: *Abortion law would suggest they want me dead too. Women aren't people. Queers aren't people. POC aren't people. The poor aren't people. I'm less fucked than you, that's for sure, but it's still pretty grim. I don't like to admit this, but I'm scared.*

Me: *I don't feel as bad for queers. As long as there are rich white men who are gay they have a fighting chance. Other queers have it just as bad, sadly. This makes me wanna watch* Pocahontas *and cry."*

Cann: *Yeah, rich white male gays aren't as oppressed. Do what makes you feel safe.*

We broke from texting for about an hour. I went and read all the Facebook posts, all the outrage, the justifications, the rebuttals, the complaints, the bizarre Twitter attack of Joshua Malina from *Scandal* on Twitter. I made up my mind how I felt, I texted Cann again.

July 14, 2013, 12:47 AM

Me: *My anger isn't directed at Zimmerman, it's directed toward a system which declared what he did not a crime.*

Cann: *Same. It let him get away with it.*

Me: *Check Ann Coulter's Twitter. Just do it.*[24]

Cann: *No.*

Me: *Really? Not just a peek?*

Cann: *I choose life in this instance.*

Me: *I hope I can watch as she burns in hell for all eternity.*

Cann: *God willing.*

Me: *As I am sure there is a God, I am sure she will be consumed entirely by the fires of Hell in its wrathful indulgence.*

Cann: *Amen.*

Me: *Oh God, what are we gonna do, Carol? Canada's looking better and better.*

Cann: *I'm thinking Denmark. Europe is sexier.*

Me: *True. Ehhh, sometimes. Lol. I'm guessing not all guys there resemble Beckham.*

---

[24] Google at your own will.

Cann: *Well at least it's a change of pace.*
Me: *True, you can be gay happier there.*

That's how my life was affected by Trayvon Martin. Other people told his story and they depicted his intentions, his dreams, and the meaning of his life secondhand because he could not do so for himself. Now his life and his death has everything to do with whom we created or want him to be. His existence is now an effigy for everything slaves worked for, Dr. King dreamt about, and Dr. Maya Angelou poetically advocated from the depths of their souls. Who was Trayvon Martin? He never had a chance to say.

That's why I mourn for him. He never had a chance to tell his own story. His life was not his parents' or the activists' or the bitter rage of a whole community, his life is something we'll never know, and like many of us living today, it goes by in a whisper. Are we willing to listen, or simply choose to speak over his voice for the sake of our own? We never allowed him to speak. Never afforded the opportunity. I think we all wanted something that would speak out against the injustice done to him, so we manipulated this young man's words and his images to cry out for past sorrow and those lingering in hopes that if we scream loud enough, they won't exist anymore. We know this can't be true because in 2013 an African-American boy can die for buying a bag of Skittles. The cops instructed George to stop, twice. And he still got off.

We wanted the world to see Trayvon Martin, and not to see him, but to see ourselves in his face. Are his eyes not my eyes? His hoodie not like every other sweatshirt in my closet? His youth unlike my own? Trayvon Martin never got to be himself in front of the world; he became every other black man, woman, gay person, lesbian, trans, handicapped person living in America and living scared because at any moment our lives could be taken from us and the perpetrator could get away with it. What a tough night all for a bag of Skittles?

That's why *Queen Called Bitch* means a great deal to me. I think all the time about my mortality, about what I want to leave behind, how people will remember me. I want something telling the world who I was and how I lived 'cause I don't like it when people guess and change things about me, in their memories I possibly won't turn out to be who I am in reality. I don't always know who I am. I'm still learning. It's hard, but I'm glad to say I have the opportunity. Part of why I'm telling my story is for all those black faces and lost souls who didn't get a chance to: those on the Transatlantic slave trade, Michael Brown, my grandmother, Trayvon, the transmen and women constantly in a state of peril, dying every day from the mere act of being alive. They were and are denied the most crucial element of humanism: storytelling.

I began this book at seventeen, pissed as hell I couldn't do precisely what I wanted with my life. I couldn't afford Emerson, go to Boston, or create a new identity for myself. I was firmly stuck with the old one. I wanted to shed my skin and see whom I'd become dancing under another sun. That wasn't in my cards. I wasn't supposed to change myself completely; I was to become more myself, a bolder Princess WaWa, a braver loud mouth Reba McEntire fan who is clumsy and obnoxious and a bitch. A queen bitch. And I have become myself more than I've ever have before.

Two years ago I sat down at the computer thinking my life was over, and after a couple years of that fire dying down, those same old flames resurfaced when I grasped I would be finishing this, turning twenty and graduating university in six months. This feeling of insecurity once accompanied with mental anguish and self-torment was overwhelming. That was so 2012. I'm closing this chapter; that doesn't mean I'm finished. I have ginormous dreams for myself, that doesn't mean I'm a failure because I'm not there yet, I haven't finished trying. And I'm not perfect because no one fucking needs to be. We are imperfections, the learning curve, life's big experiment, the ultimate question, all the right and wrong answers. We are loved, we are hated, we are hardship and depression, good times and wonder. I've had to see that we are life and we are death, we're permanent yet temporary, we are close yet distant, and distant when we need to be close. We are hard headed and foolish, and brilliant and nice, and each one is necessary for the other or else we cannot survive, and what would be the fucking point, anyway? We are the love of God, and that is what we are meant to share.

Trayvon Martin is now more than anyone could have ever dreamed. He's a sacrifice reminding us all we should all love each other a little more, hold one another tighter, and dream the biggest dreams while we still can, and never let anyone snatch him from us. I don't always love and respect myself like I should. I don't honor the people in my life with as much adoration and love as should be awarded. I should make my mother a crown and wash her aching feet and cracked hands from working fourteen plus hour days to provide for our family. I should forgive my father every day; the past cannot be changed, and my father has and is continually trying to. Every waking moment I should thank God for my sisters and my abilities, my basic faculties, and I should try harder to work within myself to let love in my life and let my dreams take me wherever they may lead.

I'm different yet I'm the same. I'm growing up and I don't see myself as quite that bitter anymore. I am always a work in progress, like I like it. This way I'll always have a job. And deep down I wonder if it's vain to be a fan of yourself? Is it okay to finally root for your own success and enable your heart's desire to be free to come to fruition?

Two days before my twentieth birthday at five a.m., I sit back, close my eyes, and grant the calm to lift me on the speedy winds to my favorite daydream. Like an inner mantra resounding from deep within, I close this chapter of my life, looking out onto the masses as they shout and chant amongst the thousands, "Long live the Queen!"

Twenty-Three: Ryan Murphy's Fucking Awesome

Watch *The Normal Heart*. Don't be a dick, just do it.

About the Author

Waldell Goode was born in Halifax, VA and is currently following dreams in Boston, MA.

Email: waldell.goode.12@cnu.edu
Facebook: https://www.facebook.com/waldell.goode
Twitter: https://twitter.com/lledlaw

Also Available from NineStar Press

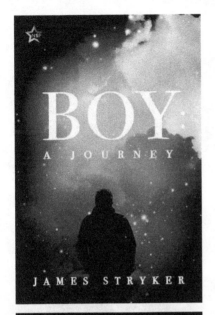

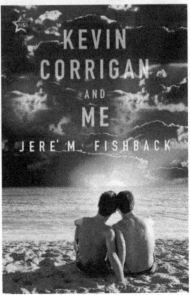

www.ninestarpress.com